晉唐以降則楷行草盛行於歷代

不多觀蓋以學書須臨三要本於

是也賓為天賦知者見多力者功深見

則變化無滯若缺天賦則研習終身化

唐法立難能可貴所以被視為傳統女

陰學書之風頗盛民間軍中皆於且其中

Frontispiece: The face of traditional China — an elderly peasant from Gansu province.
Pages 4-5: Beijing is at its best in autumn, with the gingko trees turning golden and the weather cool and pleasant.
Pages 6, 8-9: China's future and past — two bright-eyed girls in their first flush of youth
and three men in their twilight years, their life's struggle behind them.
Pages 10-11: A busy street in an old section of China's most populous city, Shanghai, which has 13 million residents.

PHOTO CREDITS

Agence ANA: 44; **Alison Wright:** 45 (bottom); **David Simson:** 45 (top); **Eye Ubiquitous:** 84, Chris Fairclough; **Photobank:** 15, 19, 20, 21 (bottom), 22-23, 24 (centre), 27 (top), 56 (top), 69 (top left), 100 (top left), 102 (top right and bottom), 105 (bottom right), 117 (top left), 120 (top right), 121 (bottom left and right), Xiaoyun; 41 (centre), 62 (centre), 87, 88, 89 (bottom), 102 (top and centre left), 107 (top right), 112 (top right above), 113 (centre), 120 (top left, bottom left and right), 121 (top), 122, 123 (top left and right), 127 (bottom right), 136, 137, 138, 139, 144, Luca Invernizzi Tettoni; 31 (top), 32, 33 (top left), 60 (centre), 68, 69 (centre and bottom left), 134, Bill Wassman; 16, 57, 64, 67 (top right), 105 (bottom left), 107 (centre), Dallas & John Heaton; 14, 46, 56 (bottom), 58-59, 103 (centre left), Pictor; 91 (centre left), 104, 106 (bottom), Steve Vidler; 82 (top left), 86 (top), Alain Evrard; 13, 91 (centre right below), back cover, Jean Kugler; 33 (top right), 83 (top left), Hans Kemp; 41 (top right), Manfred Gottschalk; 27 (bottom), Joseph Beck; 52 (top left), Nik Wheeler; 52 (top right), Chris Daves; 53, Ben Simmons; 65, Sylvain Grandadam; 82 (bottom right), Max Lawrence; 83 (bottom right), Pierre Antoine Donnet; 105 (top), Adina Tovy; 132-133, Lyle Lawson; **The Hutchison Library:** 35 (top left), Titus Moser; 34 (top left, centre and bottom), 76, Dave Brinicombe; 8-9, Jeremy Horner; 38 (centre), 93 (top), 96 (top), 124 (top right), 140 (top), Felix Greene; 38 (bottom right), 42, 77 (bottom), 80 (centre), Trevor Page; 43 (centre left), 91 (top), Melanie Friend; 43 (centre right); 48 (top left), 62 (top left), 69 (top right below), 70-71, 77 (centre), 143, Sarah Herrington; 52 (bottom left), John Hart; 69 (bottom right); 72, Nigel Sitwell; 74 (top), Bernard Regent; 95 (top); 96 (bottom), 100 (bottom), 111 (top right), Christine Pemberton; 101; 103 (bottom); 107 (top left), Mick Csaky; 108 (top); 118 (top right), J.G. Fuller; 118 (centre), 119, Lesley Nelson; 124 (top right), 140 (bottom); **Trip Photographic Library:** 10-11, 79 (bottom), 97 (top right), 114 (bottom), F. Good; 30, 33 (centre right), 39 (centre left), 83 (centre), 100 (centre), J. Sweeney; 49, 117 (top right), H. Rogers; 55 (top), 82 (top left), 91 (bottom right), J. Batten; 62 (bottom left); 66 (centre left and right); 69 (top right above), 83 (bottom left), 89 (top left), 92, 93 (bottom), 97 (top left), K. Cardwell; 73 (centre left), B. Vikander; 80 (bottom right), 86 (centre), J. Moscrop; 123 (bottom right), P. Mitchell; 124 (bottom left), Terry Wright; **Bes Stock:** 33 (centre left and bottom), 127 (top right), Hiro Miyazawa; 4-5, 6, 66 (top left), 67 (centre right), 69 (centre right), 85 (top right), 86 (bottom left), 105 (top and centre), Jill Gocher; 43 (top right), 45 (centre), 47, 50-51, 66 (bottom right); 85 (bottom right); 85 (top left); 85 (centre), Alain Evrard; 103 (centre); 107 (bottom); 113 (top and bottom); 127 (centre);130-131; **Topham Picturepoint:** 12, 24 (bottom), 26, 35 (bottom), 39 (top), 48 (top left), 54, 55 (centre), 67 (bottom), 73 (centre right and bottom), 77 (top), 86 (bottom right top), 89 (centre), 112 (top right below), 114 (top), 116, 123 (bottom left); 124 (bottom right); 125 (top right); 129; 135; 141; **Dave G. Houser:** 35 (top right), 36 (top left and bottom right), 43 (bottom left and right), 63, William Wheeler; 52 (centre right), 62 (bottom right), 75, 142, Steve Cohen; 74 (centre), 81 top), Jan Butchofsky; 80 (top left); 81 (bottom left and right); 118 (top left), James C. Simmons; **Graham Uden Photography:** 25, 40,73 (top left), 79 (top right), 94, 95 (bottom left and right), 98, 99, 103 (top left), 108-109, 110 (top), 112 (bottom), 114 (centre), 115 (centre), 125 (top left), 126, 127 (top left); **Chris Davis:** 55 (bottom), 60 (top left and right, bottom right), 66 (bottom left), 78, 86 (bottom right below), 112 (top left), 115 (bottom), 117 (bottom); 127 (bottom left); **Mark Graham:** 2, 31 (bottom), 36 (centre left), 37, 39 (centre right and bottom), 52 (bottom right), 66 (top centre and middle centre); 73 (top right), 79 (centre), 85 (bottom), 97 (bottom), 125 (bottom); **Richard I'Anson:** 28-29, 31 (bottom below right), 38 (top left and right, bottom left), 60 (bottom left), 62 (top right), 90; **Axiom Photographic Agency:** 24 (top), Luke White; 31 (bottom left), 115 (top right), Jim Holmes; 61, 115 (top left), Gordon D. R. Clements; **Jim Goodman:** 18, 31 (bottom top right), 48 (top left), 80 (bottom left), 89 (top right; **Ron Emmons:** 67 (top left), 83 (top right), 110 (top left), 124 (top left); **Life File:** 1, Stuart Norgrove; 34 (top right), 36 (top right and bottom left), 79 (top left), Richard Powers; **Focus Team–Italy:** 74 (bottom), 97 (centre), 118 (bottom); **Liba Taylor:** 41 (top left), 91 (centre right top); **CS-SIP Development Co:** 110 (bottom), 111 (top centre and below); **International Photobank:** cover, 103 (top right); **Travel Ink:** 41 (bottom), Abbie Enock.

Series Editor: K E Tan
Designer: Tuck Loong
Picture Researcher: Susan Jane A. Manuel
Production Manager: Anthoney Chua
Printed in Singapore

© 1998 Times Editions Private Limited
© 2004 Marshall Cavendish International (Asia) Private Limited

First published in 1998. Reprinted 2004

Published by Times Editions – Marshall Cavendish
An imprint of Marshall Cavendish International (Asia) Private Limited
A member of the Times Publishing Limited
Times Centre, 1 New Industrial Road, Singapore 536196. Tel: (65) 6213 9288 Fax: (65) 6285 4871
E-mail: te@sg.marshallcavendish.com Online Bookstore: http://www.timesone.com.sg/te

Malaysian Office:
Federal Publications Sdn Berhad (General & Reference Publishing) (3024-D)
Times Subang, Lot 46, Persiaran Teknologi Subang, Subang Hi-Tech Industrial Park, Batu Tiga,
40000 Shah Alam, Selangor Darul Ehsan, Malaysia.
Tel: (603) 5635 2191 Fax: (603) 5635 2706 E-mail: cchong@tpg.com.my

National Library Board (Singapore) Cataloguing in Publication Data
Wu, Rui Lian.
China :- the Middle Kingdom /- text, Wu Rui Lian. – Singapore :- Times Editions,- 2004.
p. cm.
Reprint. First published in 1998.
ISBN : 981-232-888-2
1. China-—Description and travel. 2. China—History. 3. China—Antiquities. I. Title.
DS706
951.05— dc21   SLS2004019708

CHINA
THE MIDDLE KINGDOM

CHINA
THE MIDDLE KINGDOM

Text
WU RUI LIAN

TIMES EDITIONS

CONTENTS

INTRODUCTION

C hina, the millenium's newest rising star on the world stage, is also the oldest continuous
civilization of the world. It stands poised to take an important place in the community of nations
as a superpower, even though the country, containing one-fifth of humanity, is not the Middle
Kingdom, or Zhongguo, as the Chinese have always known it.

As a measure of the antiquity of the Chinese civilization, its form of writing, a complex system of
ideographic and pictographic symbols that began developing at least 3,600 years ago, bears greater
resemblance to the now-defunct writings of the ancient Egyptians and Mayans than it does to other
writings of today. And as a measure of the country's influence, even though it was never at the centre
of the lands under heaven, as the Chinese had believed, this system of writing is used by other East
Asian peoples, such as the Japanese and the Koreans. Confucianism, a Chinese system of thought that
grew out of a chaotic period of the country's history more than 2,000 years ago, has influenced many
Asian societies and still does today. Even the West has borrowed from China, without always realizing
it. China gave the world the mariner's compass, gunpowder, paper, and even the washboard. The
census, an important tool of modern governments in social and economic planning, was first taken
during the Han dynasty some 2,000 years ago, and was first adopted by the French in the 17th century.

Yet a nation could never be great if it did not learnt from others, and China, through its long
history, has assimilated foreign cultures. For example, Buddhism, a religion that came from India, has
had a profound influence on Chinese intellectual life, and it has both enriched and overturned Chinese
religious, philosophical, literary and artistic traditions. Today, in Sichuan province, where one of
China's greatest engineering feats, the Dujiangyan, a complex irrigation system that was built more
than 2,000 years ago, still functions, there will rise another monumental engineering work, the Three
Gorges Dam, with the help of foreign technology and money.

But China's contacts with foreigners were not always happy ones, with some bringing opportunities,
but others humiliation. During the late 19th and early 20th centuries, foreign intrusion, together with
natural disasters and internal strife, brought the already weakening Qing dynasty to its knees. China
came to be known as the "sick man of Asia", its economy in tatters, its territory carved up by foreign
powers like a melon, the central government almost non-existent and the people desperately poor.

It has taken almost a hundred years for the Chinese — the stoic peasant, shrewd businessman,
idealistic scholar — to pull their country out of that abyss, years not without mistakes and blind alleys,
pain and despair. Today, the descendants of the dragon, as the Chinese call themselves, have opened
themselves up once again to foreigners, learning feverishly from them, playing catch-up with the rest
of the world. Yet, they are mindful of the rich heritage of their chequered past, as they till the same land
that they have tilled for four millennia and as they send their satellites out into space.

*Perhaps the greatest monument of China is the Great Wall whose construction began in the 7th century B.C.
Once believed to be the only man-made structure visible from the moon, the wall extends for some 10,000 km
across northern China (left). Just as equally riveting and fascinating are many of China's natural landscapes, such
as the enchanting limestone pinnacles of Guilin (above).*

HISTORY AND THE CHINESE

The Chinese are proud of what they describe as their 5,000 years of history, and no wonder, for theirs is one of the world's oldest civilizations. They have always had a passion for history, and from the moment a script was invented, had started to compile records of events. It is said that the Chinese have no epics and few creation stories, only history, not an objective one, but an endless morality tale, to which they look for a sense of direction and of duty in life.

Their early history begins in a period shrouded in myth, when legendary figures invented techniques and implements useful to men. Thus, mythical sage-emperors such as Shen Nong invented agriculture and herbal medicine, Huangdi invented writing and weapons and Yu tamed the floods.

We do know that by 5000 B.C., settlements had begun to appear along the Yellow River, where the people lived in houses of earth and wood and made tools with polished stones and pottery decorated with motifs of fish and birds.

The first recorded Chinese dynasty is the Xia (2200 -1700 B.C.), but it is only recently that new archaeological findings indicate that it might have existed. During this period, the Chinese had begun ancestor worship, the offer of sacrifices to the dead to make sure they had a happy afterlife, a practice that is continued to this day. Only male descendants could make these sacrifices, so having a son was very important. This has meant the oppression of women throughout Chinese history, and many Chinese today still favour the male child.

During the Shang (1700-1100 B.C.) dynasty, which followed the Xia, great strides were made in technology, and people wove silk and made vessels, tools and musical instruments of bronze. They lived in walled cities and grew millet, sorghum, wheat and rice. They also began to write, on bone, tortoise shell and bronze. Archaeological findings show that the Shangs used fast horse-drawn chariots for warfare and hunting and cowrie shells as money. Rulers were buried not only with their chariots, ritual bronzes and other articles of value and use, but also with human sacrifices. The rulers of Shang began as shamans mediating between the people and their gods, but through the centuries grew to become rulers of great authority far removed from their subjects.

The Zhous overthrew the Shangs in 1100 B.C., and their empire grew to spread throughout the plains of north China. This meant that rulers could no longer keep direct control over their subjects, and so began to delegate authority to relatives and friendly nobles, giving rise to a feudalistic state. These fiefs gradually began to exert their independence and to fight each other for power, with the result that the central government was greatly weakened. It was a period of political intrigue and instability, during which foreign invaders from the north also threatened the dynasty, but also one of intellectual ferment and vigorous literary development.

A philosopher who was to have great influence not only over the Chinese, but several other Asian societies, Confucius, lived during this period, known as the Spring and Autumn period (770-453 B.C.).

Tombs of the ancients reveal bits of their culture. The life-sized terracotta warriors (left), dubbed the Eighth Wonder of the World, were found buried in the tomb of the First Emperor of China, Qin Shihuang, who unified China in 221 B.C. Above: Stone animals guard the spirit road that leads to a royal Ming tomb outside Beijing.

Living in a period of turmoil, he believed that to return to the earlier state of peace and order, people had to return to the practices of the past. He taught about right relationships between people to achieve harmony: the ruled must obey the ruler, the son should obey the father, the wife obey the husband and the younger brother obey the older brother. On the other hand, the person in authority was expected to be just and reasonable. Thus, it was the people's right to overthrow an unjust ruler, and throughout Chinese history, revolts against bad rulers were to occur again and again.

The period of the Warring States (453-221 B.C.) followed, so named because of incessant warring. It was also marked by a proliferation of schools of thought including legalism and Daoism, and by technological innovation, including the use of iron, perhaps through the necessity of war. Great poetry was also written, and the work of poet Chu Yuan, *Li Sao* or the *Lament*, is still read today.

In 221 B.C., the ruler of Qin finally defeated the other states and gave himself the title of Qin Shihuang or First Emperor of Qin. He held power in his own hands, establishing a bureaucracy which he headed. This system of centralized rule was to endure for more than 2,000 years. A ruthless dictator, he consolidated his rule by burying scholars alive who disagreed with him and burning books containing views contrary to his, including those of Confucius. Men were forced into labour to build roads and canals and the Great Wall to keep out invading tribes. But Qin Shihuang also standardized weights and measures and the written language. He died in 210 B.C., and shortly after, his dynasty was overthrown.

Liu Bang, the rebel leader who established the Han dynasty (206 B.C. - A.D. 220), knew that a country could not be ruled from the back of a fighting horse, and he established a political and administrative machinery, which was similar to that under the Qin, and encouraged learning. During the Han dynasty, the centralized government was firmly established, based on the Confucian ideology of paternalistic rule by superior, educated and moral men. Examinations were instituted to pick these scholar-officials, who had to study Confucian classics. This period also saw China's borders stretching from the Pamirs in today's Afghanistan in the west to Korea in the east, and from Mongolia in the north to Vietnam in the south. The Chinese began trading with states as far away as in Europe through middlemen travelling the Silk Road, and through trade came foreign influences, including Buddhism, which was introduced from India. The Chinese invented paper and used water clocks to tell time. But stability gave way to unrest as the emergence of big estates forced peasants off the land and heavy

The portrait of the founder of Communist China, Mao Zedong (above), overlooks the enormous Tiananmen Square, outside the Forbidden City in Beijing. The square has seen many momentous events in China's recent history. On May 4, 1919, students marched to this square to protest the Treaty of Versailles, sparking a modernization movement, and it was here on October 1, 1949, that Mao proclaimed the founding of the People's Republic of China. On June 4, 1989, soldiers moved in on thousands of demonstrating students, killing several and causing a setback in China's relations with the West.

taxation impoverished the people. Peasant revolts occurred towards the end of the dynasty, which descended into disunion.

The Tang dynasty (A.D. 618-907) that followed was a splendid era of prosperity, freedom and gaiety, during which art, music and literature flourished. Buddhism began to have an influence on the people, changing their old ways of thinking. The Chinese began to open up their southern regions, hitherto a largely unexplored mass of jungles and green coastlines. They learnt to eat bananas and lichees, captured turtles in the sea to make soup, and fashioned furniture out of the liana vines of the tropical forest.

The Tang gave way to a much weaker Song dynasty (960-1279), whose frontiers also shrank. But commerce grew during this period and merchant ships sailed to Japan, the Malay archipelago and India. Paper money began to be used and progress was made in agriculture. The arts continued to flourish, including the development of the Song *ci* or poetry written to music. But the soldiers of the weak and decadent Song rulers were no match for the organized and determined Mongolian armies, and China fell to the invaders from the north.

Mongol rule under the Yuan dynasty (1279-1368) lasted no more than a hundred years before it was overthrown, again by peasants. The high point of the Ming dynasty (1368-1644) that followed was the great voyages of the eunuch Zhenghe who travelled as far as East Africa in huge ocean-going junks.

After the Ming, China once again fell to invaders from the north, this time the Manchus, who established the Qing dynasty (1644-1911) and assimilated Chinese culture at the same time as they imposed some of their cultural practices on the Chinese, including the wearing of the queue or pigtail by men. During the reign of the early Qing rulers, China prospered and expanded, and Jesuit priests worked in the royal courts as interpreters, cartographers and teachers. But during the last 100 years of Qing rule, China, once a great empire, descended into extreme poverty and want, its people ravaged by the drug opium, its territories encroached by Western powers and its rulers weak, ineffective and corrupt. It became the "sick man of Asia". Again, peasant revolts occurred.

But it was a revolutionary movement, started by a mild-mannered doctor, Sun Yatsen, which overthrew the Qing in 1911, ending centuries of imperial rule and establishing a republic. The Nationalist government, however, was weak, and much of the country was in the hands of local warlords who exploited the people. It was during this time that an intellectual movement opposing Chinese traditions and encouraging the study of Western ideas grew. One of the ideas that caught the people's imagination was socialism, and the Communist movement was born. The Nationalists and Communists cooperated to suppress the warlords in 1926, but after that, the Nationalists turned on the Communists. The two sides cooperated once again during the Second World War to fight against the Japanese who had overrun the country, but immediately after the world war ended, the Nationalists and the Communists started fighting each other again.

In 1949, the Nationalists were defeated and retreated to Taiwan island, and the Communists established the People's Republic of China. The Chinese, under the charismatic leadership of Mao Zedong, went through a rollercoaster ride of upheavals, climbing to a peak of rebuilding fervour during the Great Leap Forward in the 1950s and plunging into depths of despair during the Cultural Revolution. The great experiments of the Great Leap Forward to speed up agricultural growth and social development failed miserably, leading to a famine that killed 30 million people. And as the world marched forward, the Chinese expended further energy chasing past ghosts during the Cultural Revolution, destroying cultural artefacts and persecuting people who were believed to be clinging to old values and thoughts, hounding many to death.

China emerged from the dark days after the death of Mao in 1976, and reforms were launched to propel the country into the modern world. As the architect of the reforms, Deng Xiaoping, said, socialists should not live in poverty.

But one of the momentous events of the 20th century must be the return of Hong Kong to China on July 1, 1997, after more than 150 years under British rule. The handover washed away China's humiliation of being brought to its knees during the turn of the century by foreign powers, and its people, to paraphrase Mao, really stood up.

PART ONE
THE LAND

T hink China, and the first image that comes to mind is green paddy fields and men and women in conical straw hats, ankle-deep in water, bent double, planting rice seedlings. This is but one facet of a vast country which contains the widest range of landscapes, and one of the greatest climatic extremes in the world. China's climatic range is so great that in January, while someone may be bundled up in thick winter clothing, shovelling snow from his door stoop in the northeastern province of Heilongjiang, his friend in Hainan island is barefoot in the fields, bending to the hoe. And contrary to impression, a large part of the country consists of deserts and mountains, with only 10 per cent of the land cultivable.

To its west, rising more than 4,116 m above sea level, is the rugged Qinghai-Tibetan Plateau, crisscrossed by snowcapped peaks and glaciers. The highest plateau on earth, it is dubbed the Roof of the World. It is cold and inhospitable, and people here eke out a meagre living growing a hardy form of barley and raising animals such as the all-purpose yak. To the northwest are vast tracts of barren desert lands, largely uninhabited except in the pockets of oases. Northwards, we find the open grasslands of Mongolia, important for sheep rearing, and the windswept Loess Plateau, once an important agricultural area because of the rich loess soil, but now one of China's most fragile environments because of soil erosion and water loss.

To the northeast, a semi-circle of mountains surround the largest plain of China, where the weather can be bitterly cold in winter, dipping to as low as minus 30° C, and there is frost for four to six months of the year. But it is warm in summer, reaching a mean temperature of 20° C. It is an important agricultural area, but there are some tribes here which live by hunting and fishing too. South of this region is the North China Plain, enriched by the fertile silt deposited by the Yellow River. It is on this rich plain that the first Chinese settled some 7,000 years ago. Southwards of here is Central China, where the mightiest river of Asia, the Yangzi, flows from the mountains of Tibet in the west into the Pacific Ocean in the east, cutting China into two.

Here, warmer and wetter than the north, with mild winters and hot, humid summers, the flat, fertile plains of the Yangzi are the most agriculturally productive region of China. The mild sub-tropical climate makes it possible to raise two or three crops a year.

South of the central plains, the terrain becomes hilly again, and although there is abundant rainfall and warm climate, the rugged terrain, particularly in the southwest, makes farming difficult. Here are found rice terraces cut into hillsides and tea gardens. The southernmost regions of China, including the island of Hainan, are tropical in climate, warm and humid all year round.

On this vast and varied land, a resilient people have lived for thousands of years, adapting to its different demands and rhythms, living in harmony with nature rather than wrestling with it.

It would seem amazing that in a country where arable land makes up only 10 per cent of the land area, most of the Chinese people make a living by farming — and this is only possible through careful management of the land and water resources. Left: A woman gathers rice seedlings for transplanting in the paddy fields. Above: The Swan Lake in Xinjiang, where the land is arid and water comes from melting snow in the mountains.

RIVERS AND MOUNTAINS

The Chinese sometimes refer to their land as *jiangshan* or "river and mountain", and their landscape painting is known as *shanshui* or "mountain and water" painting because of its predominant subjects. With good reason for China has a great many mountain ranges, from the pristine snow-capped peaks of the Himalayas in the west to the lush, green subtropical mountains of the southeast, covering 43 per cent of the land; and it has no fewer than 50,000 rivers, two of them among the world's largest, the Yellow and the Yangzi, and more than 2,000 lakes. Its major rivers originate in the mountainous west, flowing eastwards into the eastern seas. And so, when the Chinese say that something has flowed east, they mean that it is lost forever, just as water in the rivers flows relentlessly downstream eastwards, never to return.

China's Sorrow

The Yellow River or Huanghe, China's second largest at 5,464 km, takes its name from the yellow silty soil which it picks up as it flows through the Loess Plateau, giving it a yellow tinge. The river has its source in the Bayan Har Mountains in Qinghai, flowing through nine provinces and draining an area of 750,000 sq km before emptying into the Bo Hai Sea. In its upper reaches, it is a clear sparkling stream, and near Lanzhou, it is a very broad and placid river. But as it wends its way, in large snakelike bends, downstream, collecting huge amounts of silt, it often overflows its banks, causing much damage to life and property, and earning itself the sobriquet "China's sorrow".

Because of silting the river has changed course 12 times, and its riverbed is raised, so dykes have to be built to keep the water from overflowing its banks. The waters of its estuary are so thick that there is little marine life. It is even said that the carp in the river have to jump into the air to breathe. But the loess silt is immensely fertile, and people have settled here from the earliest of times, so the river is also known as the cradle of Chinese civilization.

The many moods of the Yellow River — playful, placid, reflective, wrathful — have been captured by a piano concerto, the Yellow River Concerto, which also expresses the spirit of the people who have lived, worked and struggled on the river's banks. The river is a clear stream near its source (top), but turns muddy yellow as it passes through the Loess Plateau, carrying with it the rich loess soil (left and above).

The Mighty Yangzi

"While the apes cry unceasingly on both banks of the river / The light boat has travelled a thousand mountains," wrote the great Tang poet Li Bai about a journey through the dangerous but majestic Three Gorges of the great Yangzi River. The Chinese also call their longest river, the world's third largest, simply the Changjiang or Long River. It begins as melted snow in the Tanggulu Mountains in the west, flowing through the centre of the country, cutting it in half, before entering the East China Sea near Shanghai.

The Yangzi is the lifeline of China: half the crops of China grows in its river valley and people fish in its waters; it is an important transport artery, with many ships moving people and goods up and down it; and it provides 40 per cent of the country's hydroelectric power, with the promise of even more with the building of the Three Gorges Dam. But the mighty river also flows through some of the most spectacular landscapes of China. In the Hengduan Mountains between Sichuan and Tibet, its turbulent flow has cut a deep and stunning valley, and in Yunnan, it roars through a precipitous canyon called Hutiao or Leaping Tiger. In Sichuan, it cuts deeply into the limestone, creating many gorges, the most spectacular of which are the Qutang, Wuxia and Xiling, collectively known as the Three Gorges.

Motorized boats have meant that travel through the beautiful but sometimes treacherous gorges of the Yangzi River (preceding spread and left) has been made much easier. In the past, boats going upriver at some points had to be pulled by gangs of men using thick ropes, on either side of the river. A large boat might require as many as four hundred pullers, as well as a team of swimmers to loosen rope that snagged on the rocks.

Running as it does across China's middle, the Yangzi is an important transport artery, moving produce from the interior provinces to the ports on the eastern coast for export, and taking supplies to these same provinces (top and right). Above: The river begins as melting snow in the Qinghai-Tibetan plateau.

Sacred Mountains

Mountains have a special place in Chinese belief, for their heights suggest that they are closer to heaven and the gods. A mountain may even be a home of a god or a god itself. In any case, because of their remoteness from the hurly-burly world, religious practitioners through the ages have retreated to the mountains to meditate and pray, and China's mountains are dotted with temples and monasteries.

The most important of these are the Five Holy Mountains of the Daoists and the Four Sacred Mountains of the Buddhists. The Five Holy Mountains represent the five directions, north, south, east, west and centre, with the most famous being Taishan or Honourable Mountain, in the east. Some of the greatest emperors, including Qin Shihuang, journeyed to its summit to make sacrifices to heaven, and today, many Chinese make a pilgrimage to the mountain, among them young couples to pray for a male child, and old women, who think nothing of climbing its 6,293 steps through the night to the summit to see the sun rise. For the Buddhists, each of the Four Sacred Mountains is believed to be the abode of a bodhisattva.

Enchanting Hills of Guilin

Some of the most spectacular scenery in China, the inspiration of many a Chinese landscape painter, is in the region around Guilin, in Guangxi. Here, limestone pinnacles rise sharply on the edges of the gentle Li River like "kingfisher jade hairpins", enthused a Chinese poet. Abundant rain leaves a mist over the landscape, giving it an ethereal quality and a sense of peacefulness.

Like the limestone pinnacles of Guilin (above), the majestic peaks of Huangshan or Yellow Mountain in Anhui province (left and top) have inspired Chinese poets and painters, including the Tang dynasty poet Li Bai, who wrote: "Huangshan is hundreds of thousands of feet high. / With numerous soaring peaks lotus-like. / Rock pillars shooting up to kiss empyrean roses, / Like so many lilies grown amid a sea of gold." He exaggerates of course, as the highest peak, Lotus Flower Peak, is only about 1,860 metres high. But the jagged peaks amid swirling clouds and ancient pines clinging to the rock face are a sight to behold.

Roof of the World

The rugged, sombre beauty of the Qinghai-Tibetan Plateau is awe-inspiring, with pristine snow-clad peaks, craggy, barren rocks, glaciers and the blue, blue sky. But up close, this Shangri-la of foreigners' imagination is bitterly cold, the air so thin that it leaves the newcomer sick for want of oxygen, and the harsh land miserly and unyielding to the people working it. It takes great patience, persistence and a certain toughness — or is it foolhardiness? — to live on this land. It is a hard scrabble life, but the Tibetans who live in this desolate part of China have kept their humour. The poverty, grime and squalor are offset by their ruddy cheeks, their wide grins and the bright hues of their clothes. Perhaps, what has sustained them in their extremely inhospitable land is their spirituality — they are deeply religious, practising a mystic form of Buddhism called Lamaism. Tibetans grow a hardy form of barley and raise cattle. Farmers are sedentary, but some herdsmen are nomadic.

Preceding spread: Overlooking the Tibetan capital of Lhasa, on a rocky mount, is the imposing Potala Palace, once the seat of the Tibetan government and the winter residence of the Dalai Lama, who now lives in exile in India. The present complex dates from the 17th century, and consists of thousands of rooms, shrines and statues, visited daily by chanting and prostrating pilgrims who make offerings of yak butter and ceremonial scarves.

Religion (facing page) provides spiritual succour to the people, but the hardy yak (top and above) and highland barley (above left) nourish their bodies. Tibetan women may work like beasts of burden, but they are not without normal human vanity (far left and bottom left), favouring bright colours for clothes, and jewellery.

Tibetans who raise sheep and cattle, like their Mongolian counterparts, drive their herds between winter and summer pastures. They lead a nomadic life that is spent mostly outdoors, carrying their portable homes, round tents, wherever they go (this and facing page, top).

Children of the grasslands, these young girls have known only a life constantly on the move since birth (above). Right: A community of yurts. Below: Two horsemen surveying the open pastureland on which their cattle will graze.

Nomads of Mongolia

An ancient poem goes: "When the wind blows, the grasses bow down, and the sheep and cattle come into view." The wild grasses of the open Mongolian steppe grow very tall. Here, on the vast tracts of natural pastureland crisscrossed by rivers and dotted by clear lakes, Mongolian nomads drive their cattle and sheep from pasture to pasture. They live in tents called yurt, which are round so the winds of the open land won't blow them down, made of felt to protect the inhabitants from the winter cold, and with skylights at the top which provide ventilation. In summer, the base of the yurt can be lifted to let in the cool breeze.

Mongolians grow up on horsebacks and are good sportsmen, enjoying archery and wrestling. They lead a rough and tumble life, but they also love music and dance. Their singing is sonorous, bold, passionate and unconstrained and their dances lively, reflecting their candour and warmth.

GRASSLANDS AND DESERTS

To the northwest of China, reaching towards the outer edges of the country, are barren desert lands and more mountain ranges. Here is the Tarim Basin (Tarim meaning converging rivers in Uighur), crisscrossed by various rivers fed by mountain snow. People have settled on the fertile banks of the rivers and there are even forests of poplar in the midst of yellow sands. China's largest desert, the Taklimakan, is located in its west, a place so hot that when it rains, the raindrops never touch the ground because of evaporation. East of the Tarim is the Qaidam Basin — a dried up salt lake on which nothing grows, and where houses of temporary workers are built of salt. But melting snow from the surrounding mountains means that agriculture on its edges is possible. Further east, the unrelenting heat and sand give way to a sea of green — the grasslands of the Mongolian steppes, where nomads live by raising cattle.

The Taklimakan desert (below) is China's largest, a hot and desolate place with only the scorching sun and treacherous dunes, and devoid of inhabitants, although merchants with their camel caravans still traverse it as they have done since time immemorial.

Kashgar (top, right and facing page, top), the fabled ancient city where the northern and southern silk routes joined, is today still an important transport centre despite its remoteness, sited as it is by the Karakoram Highway linking China and Pakistan. It became a centre of Islam during the 10th century, and the biggest mosque in Xinjiang, the Id Kah Mosque, is found here.

Life in the "New Dominions"

The deserts may be inhospitable, but their oases are fertile, and people have settled there from the earliest of times. Among them, the largest group today is the Uighurs, who were nomads at first, but are now mainly farmers, cultivating fruit and grain and raising sheep and horses on land irrigated by underground channels of water known as *karez* — to prevent evaporation in the hot, dry weather. Their square houses of mud-bricks are dark and cool inside, with a yard overhung with grapevine to provide both shade and fruit. Their markets are colourful and lively affairs, with camels, horses, donkeys, goats, furniture, boots, hats, bright silks and cottons, dried raisins and sultanas, flat bread loaves, mutton kebabs, mutton pasties, you name it, on sale. The Uighurs are Muslims, and men wear skull caps, while women chiffon headscarves and trousers under their dresses. The ancient Silk Road of the Han and Tang dynasties threaded through this region, now known as Xinjiang or "new dominions", and some of the oasis towns, important pit stops along a hazardous trade route, contain traces from that era, including Buddhist grottoes and Chinese tombs.

Luscious, juicy fruit are always welcome to people who live in hot, dry climes. Peaches, pomegranates and grapes are just some of the fruit sold in this Kashi market, Xinjiang (left).

Uighurs mainly eat unleaven bread, although they also enjoy a bowl of noodles (above). Wheat, maize and rice are their staple grains, and on festive occasions, Uighurs serve a dish of rice cooked with mutton, carrots, raisins and onions, known as "paluo rice", to their guests. Left: A Uighur woman baking bread in an ancient clay oven.

Faces of Xinjiang: A musical instrument maker at work on a zither (right); some old-timers (centre left and facing page); and a Uighur woman with her two children (above). About half the country's Muslims, or some seven million, live in Xinjiang today.

HARNESSING NATURE

Chinese have mainly been farmers from the earliest of times. And while the ancient Babylonians and Assyrians mismanaged their water resources, deforested their catchment areas and turned their croplands into deserts, the Chinese have cultivated the same fields in some areas for more than forty centuries. They have been able to do so because they have learnt to live in harmony with nature, even as they harness it for their livelihood. They build sensible irrigation systems that have been in use for centuries, rotate their crops on the fields so that the soil is not exhausted and gather animal and human waste to fertilize their land. They light their fires with animal waste and dried grain stalks, use dried tea leaves to make pillows and threshed rice stalks to make brooms, and feed food scraps to the family pig. Nothing goes to waste and every inch of arable land is pressed into service to feed an immense population. Today, however, ancient, labour-intensive methods of farming are being replaced by modern ones, including the use of chemical fertilizers.

Many Chinese farmers still use labour-intensive methods of farming, although machinery is increasingly used. Harvesting season (above and below) is a busy time for them. Right: A woman farmer headed for the market, laden with goods for sale. Opposite top: Corn drying in a farmyard.

Chinese women work in the fields too. A woman collecting water in Dali, Yunnan (right), and three women treading on a waterwheel to draw water from a stream to irrigate their fields (far right).

Hold Back the Waters

In China's northern regions, the soil may be fertile, but the climate is harsh and fickle. Winters are long, cold and dry, during which no work on the fields is possible, and summer rains may be heavy, producing floods that wash away the crops, or erratic or scarce, causing droughts. Such natural calamities are said to hit the north once every three years. Still, the people persevere, working intensely during the warmer months, ploughing, sowing and reaping — and tending to the dykes which keep out the floods. They grow crops which thrive in dry conditions such as millet, sorghum, wheat and maize. Among them, the highest yielding is perhaps the sorghum, which grows thick and tall, and its uses are many too. This coarse grain is ground into flour to make cakes, bread and noodles or fermented to make a wine, and its stalks at one time were very important as a fuel to the northerners. No wonder that come summer, many fields are filled with what the northerners call "green gauze tents", swaying gently in the breeze.

Crops that thrive in dry conditions are grown in China's north. This grain will be used for making wine (below); two women (bottom) gathering cotton in Gansu province; and winnowing by a simple but effective method (left).

Land of Fish and Rice

China's south is often referred to as *yumizixiang*, "home of fish and rice". And no wonder, for where it is flat, the land is like an unbroken rice field, and even on the hill-slopes are rice terraces. Streams and rivers teem with marine life, but besides fishing, the Chinese have bred fish for centuries. The climate here is mild, with plenty of rain, and even in its northern parts, the winter is short, with only light snowfall, so farming takes place all year round, with, sometimes, three crops of rice in the far south. But rice is by no means the only crop, and maize is grown where irrigation is difficult. Where it is colder, winter crops such as beans are grown.

In the south, where the weather is good, farmers are busy all year round, growing more than one crop of grain a year, and tending to their vegetable plots as well (left and second from top). Besides farming, such as rice cultivation in Yunnan (top left), fishing is a common activity here, such as on the Li River in Guangxi (top right) and in Lake Dianchi in Yunnan (right). Above: A family in Fujian enjoying the evening meal in the open courtyard of their house, after a hard day's work.

Tea and Silk

Two of the world's most coveted products through the ages, tea and silk are produced mainly in China's southeastern provinces. Here, in hills on which it is difficult to grow rice, are tea and mulberry gardens, the mulberry to feed silkworms with. The quality of tea depends on the quality of land, and some tea gardens are famous for their tea. Tea leaves are prepared differently to give different types of tea: green teas are smoked, oolong teas are partly fermented and smoked and black teas are fermented. In some places, silk cultivation has been combined with fish farming for centuries, with mulberry trees planted on the edges of carp ponds and silkworms' droppings fed to the fish.

Legend has it that tea was discovered accidentally by the mythical emperor Shen Nong when a gust of wind blew some dead camellia leaves into his pot of boiling water. Today, 5,000 years on, tea is the national beverage of China. Left: Tea picking in Guizhou. Top right: A Chinese tea set.

Silk is produced using modern machinery in state factories (centre left), but it is also prepared using traditional methods in places such as Xinjiang. A Uighur man "cooking" silk (third from top right), a Uighur woman spinning silk thread (above), and another weaving silk threads into a rug (left).

CITYSCAPE

While China still remains a largely agrarian society, more and more of its teeming millions have migrated to the cities, with the result that its metropolises are bursting at the seams. China's cities are as varied as its landscape: Beijing, the capital, is staid and orderly with its wide and well-planned avenues; Guangzhou in the far south, with its raucous streets and seething mass of humanity; and Shanghai, with its freewheeling businessmen. Then there is Chongqing in Sichuan province, the wartime capital, a mountainous city understandably devoid of the usually ubiquitous bicycle brigade, with its streets narrow and winding, and cave dwellings dug out during the Second World War to shelter from Japanese bombs still in use. Hong Kong, returned to the fold of the motherland in 1997, is a financial and trading centre with a Western veneer.

The colonial Legislative Council Building and the futuristic Bank of China Tower are major tourist attractions in Hong Kong's Central district (left), while Shanghai's most distinctive landmark now is the 468-m high Oriental Pearl TV Tower (top) in Pudong Park. Beijing (above) is fast catching up with its own glass-and-steel towers, but bicyclists are still very much part of the streetscape. The highlight of Hong Kong's skyline on the waterfront in Wan Chai (right) is the state-of-the-art Hong Kong Convention and Exhibition Centre.

PART TWO

FLORA AND FAUNA

Mencius, the philosopher, wrote in 500 B.C.: "The Bull Mountain was covered by lovely trees, but it was near the capital of a great state. People came and cut the woods down and the mountain lost its beauty. Even so, the day air and the night air came to it, and rain and dew moistened it till here and there fresh shoots began to grow. But soon cattle and sheep came and grazed, and in the end the mountain became gaunt and bare as it is now. And seeing it thus, people imagine that it was woodless from the start."Deforestation has been a problem in China for a long time, as the growing population claimed every bit of cultivable land to grow food and to settle in. Despite sound environmental practices, after thousands of years of encroachment by men, China's natural heritage has become seriously depleted. Some animal species, such as the rhinoceros and the tapir, have become extinct, while others such as the South Chinese tiger and the giant panda are endangered, and the forest resources can no longer meet the country's timber needs.

Yet, China, with its great geographical and climatic variety, has a wide diversity of natural environments that contain an amazing range of plant and animal life. Its rainforests, temperate forests and grasslands hold more than 32,000 plant species, among them trees that are only found here, such as the China cypress, dawn redwood, silver fir and golden larch. China has contributed greatly to the world's larders, with crops such as the highland barley, soya beans, oilseed, rapeseed, sesame and rice having originated from here. Some of the world's favourite fruits like the orange also came from here, and the kiwi fruit or Chinese gooseberry, a major export of New Zealand, is a native of China. Its natural habitats also harbour all manner of animal life: in its desert lands are found rare animals such as the Przewalski's Horse and the Bactrian camels, while still other rare animals such as the giant panda, golden monkey and takin deer live in its forests. The Chinese river dolphin, which lives in the Yangzi River, is one of only five species of freshwater whale in the world, while the Chinese giant salamander is one of the world's largest amphibians.

While wildlife management has been a long tradition in China, 7,000 years of settlement by man has taken its toll on the land. Sound methods of farming have allowed the Chinese to cultivate the same fields for millennia, but increased use of pesticides and chemical fertilizers, some policy blunders such as the opening up of large areas of natural habitats which were unsuitable for farming, and increased pollution through the growth of towns, road construction and industrialization, have created serious environmental problems for the country. However, awareness of the need for conservation is growing, and in recent years, the country has begun to work with conservation organizations and United Nations agencies to improve its natural resource management. New laws to regulate industry to reduce pollution as well as to protect wildlife have been instituted. Some distressed habitats have been rehabilitated and several nature reserves have been set aside to protect plant and animal life.

Rising like a dragon on the Yunnan plateau is the Yulongxueshan or Jade Dragon Snow Mountain (above), so named because of the permanent snow on its highest peaks. It rises 5,500 metres above sea level and is a veritable treasure trove of plants and wildlife: the snow leopard still roams its snowy slopes and many kinds of medicinal herbs can be found here. The tiger (left) is an endangered species in China.

STEAMING JUNGLES, MAJESTIC PINES

China's physical terrain is varied and impressive. Above: The spectacular Huangguoshu falls in Guizhou province, whose thunder can be heard from a distance. Right: Green limestone hills of Yangshuo in Guangxi. Below: Pristine snow-clad peaks and pine forests of the frontier region between Yunnan and Tibet.

Extensive cultivation has meant that China's forest area is not very large — only 13 per cent of the country is covered by forest. And as most flat land and foothills have been reclaimed by men, most of the country's forests are confined to its mountains. Still, there is an enormous range of forest types, from steaming rainforests, teeming with life from the dense undergrowth to the tops of their 30 m tall trees, to the cold, majestic coniferous forests of the far north, where winters last for as long as nine months and there is permafrost, and little life beneath the tree canopy save for mosses and lichens and small shrubs on damp and boggy ground. In between are the deciduous forests and evergreen subtropical forests. Among the overwhelming number of plant species is the water larch or dawn redwood, a tree commonly found in East Asia, North America and Europe before the Ice Age, but believed to be extinct until in 1943 when some trees were discovered in Hubei province. It was honoured as a living fossil, and reintroduced to the rest of the world.

Nature Reserves

To protect what is left of its natural environment, China has set aside several hundreds of nature reserves of varying sizes, where public excess is limited and commercial exploitation or farming banned or restricted. These are picked according to different aims and objectives: some are intended to protect entire ecosystems; for example, the Changbai Mountains preserve the mountain ecosystem and landscape of the temperate zone while the Xishuangbanna reserve protects the tropical environment and its wildlife. Some are for the protection of rare animals, such as the Wolong reserve, picked for the giant panda, golden monkey, snow leopard and other rare animals that live in it. Then there are those specifically for the protection of rare and precious plants, or special geological profiles or landforms, such as the Liangshui reserve with its primeval Korean pine forests and the Wudailianchi with its volcanic landscape. There are also reserves set aside simply for their beauty, such as Jiuzhaigou in Sichuan province with its chain of lakes and waterfalls set in a forested valley surrounded by mountains.

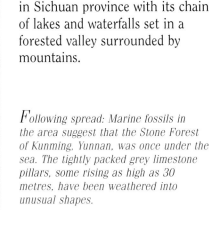

Following spread: Marine fossils in the area suggest that the Stone Forest of Kunming, Yunnan, was once under the sea. The tightly packed grey limestone pillars, some rising as high as 30 metres, have been weathered into unusual shapes.

The Ubiquitous Bamboo

If there is a plant that people associate with China, then it has to be the bamboo. Tall, slender and graceful, it is one of the favourite subjects of Chinese ink painters. China has the largest number of bamboo species in the world — of the more than 1,000 species worldwide, 300 can be found here. And it contains one-fifth of the world's total bamboo grove coverage. Bamboo is found almost throughout China, from the Yellow River in the north to Hainan island in the south and from Tibet in the west to Zhejiang in the east. Beautiful as it is, this tree-like grass is not merely ornamental. Bamboo shoots are a delicacy in Chinese cuisine and bamboo stems, strong and pliable, have been used to build houses and made into furniture, baskets and other wares since as far back as 7,000 years ago. Because of this same strength and pliability, the bamboo has come to symbolize resilience and integrity — it may bend to the wind, but it always returns to an upright position.

WILDLIFE — SURVIVING ENCROACHMENT

It is said that the Chinese eat any animal that has its back to the sky, and true enough there is a mind-blowing range of exotic meat on a Chinese menu — snake, monkey, pangolin, bear, giant salamander, raccoon, frog, you name it — reflecting the range of wildlife of the land. In addition, some animals are hunted for their perceived medicinal value, for example, deer for their antlers to treat fevers and male tigers for their penis, believed to be an aphrodisiac. Yet some are killed for their beauty, such as pheasants for their feathers. Shrinking habitats have also reduced the animals' numbers. But in the southern tropical forests, elephants still run, monkeys still swing in the trees and tigers still roar, while fleet-footed gazelles still fly across the grasslands. And in the extreme north, reindeer, moose, musk deer, bears and sables romp the forests still.

The red panda (above) bears little resemblance and is not related to the more famous giant panda (facing page). A much smaller animal, it also feeds on the stems and leaves of bamboo, as well as fruits and birds' eggs.

Some of the most unusual animals and animal parts can be found in China's markets. These are traditional medical cures, such as deer antlers, tortoiseshell, snakes and starfish (above and left), which may be decocted into a drink or made into poultices or ointments for application. Sharksfin (below) is highly valued both as a delicacy and a tonic food by the Chinese.

The Giant Panda

Playful animals that are a joy to watch, giant pandas had been the country's ambassadors, together with its ping-pong players, during the beginning of the thaw of relations between Communist China and the rest of the world in the 1970s. They can today be seen in zoos around the world. But sadly, in their natural home in the provinces of Sichuan, Shaanxi and Gansu, they are threatened with extinction because the types of bamboo leaves and stems on which they feed are getting scarcer as bamboo forests shrink.

Creatures of Intelligence — and Mischief

The monkey has been immortalized in an ancient Chinese novel, *Journey to the West*, which chronicles the journey of a Buddhist monk from China to India to obtain Buddhist scriptures. The monk is accompanied by a boar spirit, a sand spirit and a monkey spirit, with the resourceful monkey spirit always going to the rescue of his master and his other companions when they fall into trouble. But the monkey spirit is also frequently getting into scrapes himself because of his mischievous nature. The monkey as a deity in the Chinese pantheon has been accorded with great wisdom too, and is known as the Great Sage Equal to Heaven. And in the Chinese zodiac, those born in the year of the monkey are characterized as active, bright, humorous, kind, lovable, conceited, super-sensitive — and greedy for wealth. Whether the real monkey possesses all these traits is debatable, but there are several monkey species in China, the most beautiful of which must be the golden monkey, with its thick, long, golden fur.

China has one of the world's best environments for monkeys in its subtropical and tropical forests, and many species of monkeys and gibbons can be found here. They eat mainly fruit, leaves and flowers, although the slow loris, a lower primate, also eats birds' eggs and insects. The Pere David's Macaque (facing page) is considered "king of the monkeys".

The Hunter is the Hunted

China's animals of prey have been very much the hunted themselves, and several are now very rare if not close to extinction. The South Chinese tiger and its Siberian cousin are now seriously endangered, there being only about 100 Siberian tigers in China, and well under a hundred South Chinese tigers. The clouded leopard, smaller than the familiar leopard and very attractive, is now very rare, so is the snow leopard of the mountains. But the leopard cat, Asiatic golden cat and the lynx are still found in healthy numbers, although the last is hunted heavily for its fur. Out in the deserts, there are two beautiful cats, the Chinese desert cat which is adapted to burning hot summers, freezing winters and dry winds, and the Pallas's cat, a rare predator adapted to the very cold weather of the high plateaus in the desert, with its beautiful, thick coat.

A beautiful animal, the snow leopard (top) inhabits very cold regions. It hunts in isolation, and is capable of killing creatures three times its size. To withstand the cold, it has two layers of fur, a long, tough coat outside and a soft, wool-like shorter coat beneath. The Manchurian tiger (left), like its Siberian and South China cousins, is highly endangered, being much hunted. Above: A Qing dynasty painting showing a tiger hunt.

CREATURES OF THE AIR

China must have some of the world's most beautiful birds, from the hornbills and parrots of the tropical forests to the splendid pheasants and tragopans of the mountains to the cranes, herons, ibises, storks and ducks of the wetlands, many of them an inspiration to the country's painters and poets through the ages. Then there are the birds of prey, of which there are 56 species in China, including hawks, falcons and eagles. But, to the birds' misfortune, Chinese love the songbirds best, keeping them in cages so that they can hear their birdsong all day long. These include warblers, finches, thrushes, bulbuls, orioles and larks, several of them endemic species.

Fishers of the Li

Cormorants are great fishers, and the Chinese have used them for centuries to catch fish. They tie a string round the birds' neck to prevent them from swallowing the fish before setting them off from their boats to dive into the lakes or rivers. After the work is done, the birds are well rewarded for their labour from their catch. But after the Communists came into power in 1949, they banned the domestication of cormorants for fishing because they were severely depleting fish stocks! Even so, today, traditional fishing flocks are still to be seen on the Li River in Guangxi province.

Not content with hearing birdsong in the open, the Chinese have since the earliest of times kept songbirds near at hand in cages. A pet shop in Shenzhen (above), a bustling special economic zone across the border from Hong Kong, has a great variety of songbirds. Left: The heron, one of China's many bird species. Right: Cormorants fish in the evenings.

Bird of Immortality

Of the 15 species of crane worldwide, nine are found in China, where they not only breed, but also winter. For example, the rare red crown or Japanese crane breeds in places such as Inner Mongolia, Heilongjiang and Jilin and winters in the Yangzi River catchment area. With such a strong presence in the country, it is not surprising that this elegant and beautiful bird has made its way into Chinese mythology and beliefs. The crane is usually pictured carrying sages off to the Three Islands of the Immortals, and is itself a symbol of immortality for the Chinese.

HARBINGER OF PLENTY

With the country having so many rivers and lakes, fish has always been an important part of the Chinese's diet. But the Chinese eat fish not only for sustenance, but also for its symbolism, particularly during the Lunar New Year. For the word fish, or *yu*, sounds like "excess" or "plenty". And so, new year greeting cards carry pictures of fish and the greeting "nian nian you yu" or, roughly translated, "may you have excess every year". While China has a long coastline, most of its population lives inland, away from the sea, so the Chinese probably eat more freshwater fish than those from the sea. Besides catching fish, the Chinese also breed them in lake or riverside farms. The most common freshwater fish is the carp, with several species, but there are also salmon, trout, graylings and barbel. Chinese also keep fish as pets, including the goldfish, which originated in the rivers of eastern China.

A Chinese pond is never quite complete without golden carp, water lilies and weeping willows (top left).
Top right and above: Bringing in the catch on the coast of the Yalong Bay on Hainan island; and fishermen using fish traps on the Erhai Lake in Dali, Yunnan province. Facing page and right: The Chinese like to eat their fish fresh and usually buy their fish at the market for cooking on the same day. They even buy their fish live sometimes. But they also eat dried, salted fish, usually with rice porridge at breakfast. Here a stall in Qingdao, Shandong province, sells dried fish (far right).

ANIMALS AND DOMESTICATION

Even before the inhabitants of China began to cultivate crops, they had begun to domesticate animals, such as dogs, during the Old Stone Age, more than 30,000 years ago. Later, during the New Stone Age, pigs, sheep, cattle, horses, chickens, ducks, yaks and camels became widely reared, and still are today. These animals are reared for food or for their hide or as draught animals, or a combination of the three. For example, the long-haired, hardy yak, known as the "boat on the plateau", is used by the Tibetans to carry heavy loads and as a source of meat, milk, butter and cheese, and of wool.

Chinese domesticate animals to provide food, labour and pelts, but also for sport and as a hobby. A Kazakh horseman with his hunting falcon (top left), a yak being loaded with a harvest of wheat (top right), herdsmen with their some of their herd (centre), a farmer with his trusty oxen (above), sitting pretty in a donkey cart (right) and two Bactrian camels (facing page), a very rare sight now in China.

PART THREE

PEOPLE, CUSTOMS AND BELIEFS

Chinese are an exuberant lot: their streets are raucous; in their restaurants, waiters try to outshout the diners; at the opera, they eat their nuts and seeds noisily and shout words of approval when they have enjoyed a particular scene; at funerals, it is expected of mourners to wail loudly; and they celebrate occasions with noisy lion dances and a burst of firecrackers. All this simply reflects a zest for life.

People have accused the Chinese of being practical and utilitarian to a fault, but this is borne of an ideal that life is to be enjoyed. They are all too aware of the fleetingness of happiness: living through hard times of war and pestilence, natural calamities and misrule has made sure of that. And so they do all they can to secure a good life, applying to the gods for fortune, good health — and male descendants, so as to have a good afterlife, for then there will be someone to offer them food and burn paper money and clothes for their use in the Yellow Springs, where one goes to after death. They strive to live in harmony with nature, in order not to incur its wrath and so bring on natural disasters, consulting their almanac before they do anything important such as getting married or opening a business or simply moving house. They also work hard and are a frugal people, especially when they are just beginning to build their fortune, laying up wealth so that their descendants may not go hungry.

Perhaps it is because of the influence of Daoism, which stresses oneness with nature, but an ideal of happiness for the Chinese is the enjoyment of a simple rural life, as reflected in this 16th century poem: "Life is complete with children at your feet; just a handful of hay hides your cot. If land is sterile, to make it fertile, a young calf will surely help a lot. Teach thy sons to read, too, in spare hours, not for fame nor for Mandarin collars. Brew your wine, plant bamboos, water flowers, thus a house for generations of scholars". While today such a life is not possible in the cities, people take every opportunity to escape the grime and closeness of their surroundings into nearby hills and open areas, particularly in spring. There is even a festival for hill trekking.

In the quest for happiness, nothing is perhaps more important than the family and the harmony within it. The Chinese have a saying: "When the family is in harmony, all things thrive." Duty towards the family is paramount, sometimes at the expense of personal happiness. The family institution is enhanced by the practice of ancestor worship, offerings and prayers to the dead, usually the duty of the male descendant. It is also expected of the son to take care of the parents in their old age. While the extended family of old, in which a patriarch lives with his sons and their families, exists now only in the countryside, in the city, many families are still three-generational, with grandparents, parents and children living under one roof.

Life for the old folk in China (left) is not lonely as they usually live with their children's family. For young children, particularly in the urban areas, life revolves around school (above), with after-school hours mostly spent on homework. But they also join clubs and associations for hobbies.

NOT QUITE ONE RACE

The people of China are not quite a homogeneous group — there are some 56 nationalities, of which the Han Chinese are the most numerous, making up 91.6 per cent of the population of 1.3 billion. Han Chinese live in the heartland of China, mainly along the Yellow, Yangzi and Pearl rivers, and in the northeastern plains. They are the people that foreigners know as the Chinese race. The non-Han minorities, although small in numbers, occupy some 50 per cent of the country's land area.

Although they share the same language and culture, the Han Chinese are by no means a homogeneous block. They speak different dialects, some so markedly different, that the speaker of one is unable to understand the speaker of another. Different groups also have different customs and traditions, enjoy different cuisines and even have their own style of music. To communicate, however, they use *putonghua*, a dialect of the northern region which has the largest number of native speakers. And they use a standardized form of writing.

Beneath the head of black hair and the yellow skin, the Chinese are a diverse people. The different dialects they speak are not simply regional varieties of a language — some dialects are considered to be languages in their own right. And even if they share the same religion, Daoism, people of different regions have their different favourite deities. One reason for this diversity is the many mountain ranges in the country, which made travel difficult in the past, and so isolated groups of people from one another. Facing page and this: Faces of the Han — young and old, urbanites and country folk.

Living on the Outer Edges

China's minority groups are scattered in the border regions in the north, northeast, northwest, west, southeast and southwest of the country. Most of the groups have their own spoken languages and 23 have their own written languages. The Mongolians and Kazakhs who live in the grasslands of the north and northwest are nomadic herdsmen, driving their sheep, cattle and horses between winter and summer pastures. In the northeast, the Hezhes, one of the smallest ethnic groups, live by hunting and fishing. Many of the groups who live in the south, southwest and southeast are farmers, including the Zhuangs and the Lis.

Beauty, it's in the headdress: Miao women from different subgroups dress their hair differently (top and above) — Miaos live mainly in Guizhou; a Bouyei woman from Guizhou with her intricately dressed hair (second from top); and two Tu women of Qinghai province with their colourful, brimmed hats (overleaf).

Yunnan, or "south of the clouds", in China's southwest bordering Myanmar, Laos and Vietnam, is home to almost half of the country's ethnic minorities.
Left: The old city of Lijiang in Yunnan is more than 800 years old, with narrow, winding streets of cobblestone, where older Naxi women still wear their traditional garb, although younger ones favour modern clothing.
Above: Market day in Lijiang.
Top left: Harvest time for the Lisu.
Right: A Sani woman in Kunming.
Far right: Mealtime for a Dai family.

A MOSAIC OF RELIGIOUS BELIEFS

The Chinese have always believed in a spiritual world populated by gods, spirits and fairies, which they strive to live in harmony with. This means avoiding offending them or appeasing them when they have been angered inadvertently. Or they may pray to these gods and spirits for help to have a good harvest or pass an examination. Then in the 5th century B.C., there arose two systems of thought, Confucianism and Daoism, the former reiterating moral values of the time and encouraging ancestor worship, and the latter teaching the harmonization of man with the natural order. Daoism later became a popular religion.

The first foreign religious influence was in the form of Buddhism, during the Han dynasty, followed by Christianity, and then Islam. Today, the Chinese list their main religions as Daoism, Buddhism, Islam and Christianity. But most Chinese practise an amalgam of the three teachings, Daoism, Buddhism and Confucianism — although the last is not a religion — mixed with ancient folk beliefs.

Christianity came to China as early as A.D. 635, during the Tang dynasty, via the Silk Road, but despite its long history in China, it has made little impact on the Chinese, with followers concentrated mainly in the large cities. A Catholic Church in Xiamen, Fujian (top left) and a pastor outside his church in Harbin, Heilongjiang (above).

Daoism as a popular religion is a mix of Daoist doctrines and age-old folk beliefs: The Yellow Dragon Temple in northern Sichuan (left); a woman devotee offering incense to the gods (centre left); the Temple of the Eight Immortals in Xian, Shaanxi (above) and the Green Dragon General, a Daoist deity (centre right).

Daoism — Quest for Immortality

Daoism is said to have been founded by Lao Zi, or Old Master, a legendary sage said to have lived at about the same time as Confucius. He was attributed with writing the book *Daode jing* or the *Book of the Way and its Virtue*. The Way in the pure and philosophical form of Daoism is the way of nature. The Daoist doctrine states that man should understand himself as being a part of nature, and that change is the way of everything in the universe: growth, decay and death. Man should therefore not cling on to any particular form, not even his body. Only then can he endure longer in the world or attain immortality.

Some early Daoists believed in living a hermit's life in the wilderness, but later Daoists said detachment could be found anywhere. Wrote Tao Qian, a Daoist poet of the 4th century A.D.: "I have built my hut beside a busy road but I can hear no clatter from passing carts and horses. Do you want to know how? When the mind is detached, where you are is remote also."

Daoists have developed a breathing exercise called *qigong* and a form of shadow-boxing known as *taijiquan*. They also meditate and keep a vegetarian diet, all with the aim of attaining immortality.

Buddhism — Extinguishing Desire

Buddhism was brought to China by Indian merchants via the Silk Road during the first century B.C. But it did not spread widely until after the 4th century A.D., during the Tang dynasty. Even so, the Chinese have transformed it; for example, Chan Buddhism, a form of Chinese Buddhism, is a fusion of Daoism, other Chinese beliefs and Indian Buddhism. Thus, in the main hall of a Chinese Buddhist temple, at the back of the main Buddha image, there is an image of Guanyin, the Goddess of Mercy, surrounded by a pantheon of Chinese gods and spirits.

While original Buddhists believed that enlightenment was attained through slow, careful steps, in Chan Buddhism, a Chinese form of the religion, enlightenment can come suddenly, without warning. Chan Buddhism was adopted by the Japanese, who call it Zen Buddhism. Above: The Nanputuo Temple in Xiamen, Fujian. Top: Images of the historic Buddha, Sakyamuni, in a temple in Guangzhou. Right: Devotees in a Hangzhou temple. Facing page: A monk with his prayer beads.

Islam — Pure and True

Islam was brought to China by Arab and Persian merchants, also via the Silk Road, during the Tang dynasty, at round about the 7th century A.D. Several ethnic minorities are Muslim, including the Uighurs, Kazakhs, Tajiks and Kirgizes. But the largest group of Muslims are the Huis, originally Muslims of Middle Asia who migrated to China during the 13th century, intermarried with the Chinese and adopted some Chinese cultural practices. They now speak and write the Chinese language and have even adopted Chinese names, but also adhere strictly to Muslim religious practices, such as abstinence from pork and alcohol and covering their heads. Islam is also known as *qingzhen* or "pure and true" in Chinese, and their mosques are known as *qingzhen miao* or "pure and true temple".

*T*here are Muslims throughout China, but most of them live in the provinces of Ningxia, Gansu, Qinghai, Henan, Hebei, Shandong, Yunnan and Xinjiang, with about half of them found in Xinjiang. Some of them, like the Huis, have assimilated much of Chinese culture. Facing page: An imam or Muslim religious elder in Xinjiang. This page, from top: A mosque on the bank of the Yellow River in Lanzhou, Gansu; a Hui extended family in Qinghai province — women wear the veil, but young girls do not; and men at prayer at the Id Kah Mosque in Kashgar, Xinjiang.

RITES OF PASSAGE

In the days when infant mortality was high, when a child was born, especially if it was male, it would be named after an animal, such as "pig" or "dog" or "buffalo", to hide it from the jealous gods. Today, this practice is no longer continued, but the birth of a child is no less an important event, and when the child is a month old, the family holds a celebration for family and friends. Traditionally, children's birthdays are celebrated very simply, with the eating of eggs and noodles, and offering made to the gods.

Among some Chinese, when the child reaches the age of 15, a ceremony is held to signify his or her coming of age. When it is time to marry, in the countryside, parents still make the match for their children, although in the cities, Chinese choose their own partners. Country

weddings are elaborate affairs, with many traditions still being observed, but weddings in the cities are celebrated simply with a banquet at a restaurant. Adult Chinese do not celebrate birthdays until after the children have married, when they will celebrate their parents' birthdays, and birthday food again includes eggs and noodles, as well as dumplings in the shape of peaches, all to signify long life. Chinese measure time in 60-year cycles, and completing such a cycle is an important milestone in a person's life, to be celebrated with a big banquet for friends and relatives.

Posing for a wedding picture (right). A Chinese person is never quite regarded as an adult until he or she marries. Above: A man selling red eggs. Red is the colour for luck for the Chinese, and red eggs are eaten during the celebration of a baby's first month.

The male child is still favoured, but today, with every urban family restricted to having only one child, the child, whether male or female, is doted upon by parents and grandparents alike. The terms for such indulged children are "little emperor" and "little empress". A grandfather's pride (facing page); the centre of attention (above); and street boys in Shanghai (left).

FESTIVALS OF CHINA

As the Chinese are mainly agriculturalists, many of their festivals and celebrations are connected with the natural cycle of seasons, such as *dongzi*, on the winter solstice, to celebrate the turning point of time when days get longer and nights shorter, or the mid-autumn festival which celebrates the harvest. The Chinese also celebrate the birthdays of their many gods and spirits, and have festivals to commemorate historical events or remember historical heroes or their ancestors, and even festivals to celebrate favourite myths, such as the touching love story of a cowherd and a weaver girl. While the Western calendar has been adopted for secular life, the Chinese use their own Chinese calendar, in existence for thousands of years, for important events, such as a wedding, and observance of their numerous festivals. However, many among the urban population have stopped observing many of these festivals, and they are mainly celebrated in the countryside, although there are some major ones which are still celebrated nationally.

Kumquats and Mandarin oranges are important for the celebration of the spring festival, being displayed prominently in the homes and exchanged as gifts (above). Their gold colour signify wealth for the Chinese.

Chinese festivals, whether religious or otherwise, are colourful and noisy affairs, with public performances of dragon (above) and lion (facing page, top) dances or the opera, and with celebrants decked out in their colourful best. Mosuo women in Lijiang celebrating their spring festival (right); even vendors are dressed in their best clothes during a religious festival in Yunnan (far right). In the midst of celebrating the most important Chinese festival, the Lunar New Year, the religious do not forget to offer prayers, incense and food to the gods for blessings for the year to come (facing page, bottom).

Spring Festival

There is no festival more important than the spring festival or Lunar New Year, which falls between late January and early February, during which people are given three days of public holiday. For the religious, this is a time to thank the gods for the harvest of the previous year and to pray for continued blessings in the coming year. For the not so religious, it is a great excuse to spring-clean the house, discard old things and replace damaged or worn-out ones. Preparations also include buying or making a new set of clothes, paying up debts and filling rice bins and larders to ensure a year of plenty. Perhaps the most important day of the festival is the eve of the New Year, when the family has a reunion dinner, and children living far away try to make it home for this. After dinner, the family sits together to chat or play games until the early hours to usher in the New Year. On New Year's day, people put on their new clothes to visit their friends and relatives. Children are given little red packets containing money for luck. There would be lion and dragon dances and stilt-walking performances in public places.

Remembrance Need Not Be Sombre

Solemnity and quiet are not Chinese traits, and even Chinese funerals are noisy, with wailing mourners and chanting monks. So when Chinese remember their dead, it is not a quiet, sombre affair. Qingming, or Pure Brightness Day, which occurs on April 5, is a day when people remember their dead ancestors by sweeping their tombs and paying respects to them. But it is also a time to go into the country, where tombs are sited, to enjoy the beauty of spring, so it is also known as Stepping on Greenery festival. People generally have a good time in the open.

Another festival of remembrance, the Dragon Boat festival, is also marked by gaiety. Falling on the fifth day of the fifth lunar month, it commemorates the death of a patriotic poet who drowned himself in a river when his state was conquered by another. Tradition has it that villagers threw rice dumplings into the river to prevent fish from devouring his body, then spent days trying to recover it. On the anniversary of his death, people hold dragon boat races and eat rice dumplings stuffed with meat and wrapped in bamboo leaves.

One of the highlights of summer is the dragon boat races, held to mark the anniversary of the drowning of a Chinese patriot and poet Qu Yuan (above). Right: A family paying their respects to a dead ancestor at the cemetery on Qingming day. It is a day of coming together for relatives and an outing for the children, anything but a solemn occasion.

A Touch of Colour

Festivals and celebrations of the minority groups are no less colourful or gay. In Yunnan province, the Dais have a water splashing festival in spring during which people splash water on each other to wash away bad fortune and usher in good fortune, while on the 24th day of the sixth lunar month, the Yis hold a torch festival. On this day, they carry torches round the houses and fields to drive away pests, and then gather round bonfires to sing and dance and drink wine through the night as well as to pray for a good harvest. The Ewenkis in northeast China, who are herdsmen, celebrate a festival in May during which people dressed in their holiday best go from yurt to yurt to enjoy food specially prepared for the occasion and young men show off their skills in lassoing horses, branding and castrating them. Families also count their new-born lambs and take stock of their wealth. Many minority groups are musical people, and their festivals are marked by singing and dancing.

The Miaos of Guizhou are a musical people and their festivals are marked by much dancing and singing. On their New Year, men and women, dressed in their holiday best, gather to dance (top) to the music of the lusheng (above). There are also bullfights and horse-racing. The Dais of Yunnan welcome the coming of spring by splashing water on each other (top right). Left and right: A Tibetan girl appropriately adorned for a flower festival celebration and a horse race at another Tibetan festival. The most important festival for the Tibetans is their New Year, during which people dressed in their holiday best go to the monasteries to receive blessings. On the 15th day, religious rites are held at the monasteries and Tibetan families light up butter lamps when night falls.

LIFE IN THE CITY

Women bikers in Zhengzhou (above). Women in the cities have more opportunities than their counterparts in the countryside in terms of education and career, and they have greater freedom to try new things as well.

City people enjoy better amenities than their rural cousins, with better housing, better schools, better hospitals and better recreational facilities. Both men and women work, so young children are usually left in the care of grandparents or placed in a childcare centre. Lunch breaks are long, and parents can go home to prepare lunch for their schoolgoing children. Sometimes, neighbourhood committees provide lunch for children whose parents cannot be home during the lunch break and there is no other adult at home. Until recently, people could expect to be taken care of by the state from cradle to grave, as most work in state enterprises, where employment is for life and workers and their family's welfare is taken care of, from housing to education to health care. But now, with economic reforms, the "iron rice bowl" is threatened, with these enterprises gradually being turned into private ones. Some Chinese are also working for foreign joint-venture companies where the pay is higher, but where there is no security of lifelong employment or such complete welfare benefits as the states' firms.

With many rural folk migrating to urban areas in search of a better life, China's cities are getting overcrowded, particularly metropolises like Shanghai and Beijing. Multi-level shopping centres, like this one in Guangdong province (left), are becoming a common sight. Food hawkers are very much a part of the Beijing streetscape and that of other cities (top right), as well as bicycles, seen here at rush-hour in Kunming, Yunnan (above); a family of three is now the norm in China, a result of the one-child policy (right).

The Bicycle Brigade

Each morning, hundreds of thousands of workers pour into the cities' wide boulevards and narrow lanes in a torrent on their bicycles, including carefully rouged and coiffed women in pretty dresses and high heels and men in suit and tie. Most Chinese live near their place of work and the bicycle is an adequate means of transport for them. It is also cheap. But with greater affluence, there are more cars on the streets, so that in some main streets, there are separate lanes for motorized vehicles and bicycles. Still, at traffic junctions, it is a game of dodge'ems and there is much tooting of the horn and shouting during peak hours.

Eating is Good Fortune

The Chinese say: "Fortune enters through the mouth", and indeed, food is such a passion for them that one of their stock greetings when meeting someone they know is "Have you eaten?" Chinese eat three square meals a day, and snacks in between. Their streets are filled with food stalls selling all manner of snacks, from light to heavy, hot to cold, steamed to fried. There are restaurants, teahouses, wine shops, hole-in-the-wall food outlets.

Chinese eat to stave off hunger, but also for pleasure and as a social event, with banquets being long drawn-out affairs consisting of many courses, each course consisting of several dishes of food. The staple food for northerners is wheat, which is turned into breads, noodles and dumplings, while the southerners eat mainly steamed rice. But rice is also made into cakes, noodles and biscuits.

People in different parts cook their food differently: northerners use lots of garlic, chilli and oil while those who live in the Yellow River basin like their food sweet and sour, but the most celebrated cuisines are those from the south, such as Teochew and Cantonese, which stress freshness of food cooked lightly with little seasoning.

While the better-off Chinese dine at fancy restaurants which have private rooms for their guests (top and above), ordinary folk are content with eating in the open. A breakfast outlet offering steamed dumplings, steamy hot rice porridge and youtiao, deep-fried dough fritters (right); eating nourishing duck and chicken soup in Suzhou, Jiangsu (far right, above); and a roadside stall selling dog meat (far right, bottom). Fish and shellfish have traditionally dominated the Chinese diet, with vegetables often cooked with shellfish — facing page, clockwise from top left: shellfish and mushrooms; sharksfin; steamed fish and more vegetables and shellfish; and stuffed chicken.

Tea is drunk by the Chinese throughout the day in place of water to quench thirst, but tea-drinking is a social event too. At their teahouses, where Chinese gather to drink tea and chat, many kinds of tea are served together with snacks known as dianxin, or "dot the heart". But these rich snacks of meat-filled dumplings, pastries and rice cakes (facing page) can also be eaten as a main meal, as some do, for lunch. A very basic roadside teashop (left) and a teahouse in Shanghai (below).

Chinese in different regions have their own different tea-drinking rituals, although these may not be as elaborate as the Japanese tea-drinking ceremony, the chanoyu. Above: A young child's initiation into the art of tea-drinking.

Food as Medicine

As with other aspects of life, Chinese seek harmony through the food they eat. They believe that the natural world possesses two opposing qualities, yin and yang, seen in decay and growth, night and day, cold and heat, female and male. These qualities are not static, and so night follows day, and nothing is totally yin or totally yang.

To achieve harmony, one should seek a balance between the two, and so everyday food is eaten to keep this balance in the human body, for example, green vegetables, which are yin, are balanced with meat, which is yang. When a person falls ill, it is because the body is not in balance, and so herbal brews are imbibed to correct this. For example, if one has a sore throat, it means the body is too yang, and cooling teas like chrysanthemum should be taken. Or if one has a stomachache, one is too yin, and ginger tea should be taken to correct this. Or if they are weak or tired, they might take some tonic food such as ginseng to perk them up and give them energy.

Time for a Breather

After the day's work is done, there are many ways city people can unwind: they can go to the cinema or a karaoke bar or enjoy a meal out or simply watch television at home. Or they may go bowling or the disco or ballroom dancing, the last a favourite pastime of older people. On some evenings, sections of streets are closed to traffic for ballroom dancing and other recreational activities, including karaoke singing. Older people also like a game of mahjong or cards or chess. Chinese like visiting relatives and friends for a chat over tea and snacks, and they usually do so unannounced. And city parks are always filled: with people exercising in the mornings, old folk to meet their friends for a game of chess or cards or just to chat, keepers of songbirds, lovers in the evenings, and picnicking families on weekends.

China at rest: Elephant chess at a Chengdu park, facing page; this page, clockwise from top — A game of mahjong, now officially a national sport; chat time; an island of quiet on a bustling street; avid comic readers at their favourite comics rental library; birdsong goes well with tea; and ballroom dancing on the Bund in Shanghai.

Martial Arts

The people seen doing their exercises in the parks are not practising aerobics, but ancient exercises that Chinese have been doing for centuries. These are usually *taijiquan*, or shadow-boxing, or *qigong*, a form of breathing exercises. In *taijiquan*, the mind guides the body through slow, gentle but firm movements, which are combined with deep breathing. The result is a feeling of calmness. *Qigong* is supposed to help a person keep alert, live longer and overcome illness.

While jogging and aerobics are growing in popularity, most Chinese still do traditional exercises developed over thousands of years by the Daoists to keep the body healthy and to prolong life, such as taijiquan *and* qigong. *In the mornings and evenings, people young and old can be seen in the parks, outside their apartment blocks or shops and offices, in school and factory compounds, or simply an open ground (left and above) going through their paces.*

RURAL RHYTHMS

Life in the countryside is simpler, with fewer distractions unlike in the city. But it is a hard life, with farm work claiming most of the people's time. In the evenings, adults may play a hand of cards and the younger ones go to a travelling cinema. But the industrious may spend the evening sewing blankets or weaving baskets for sale. Those who live near towns may make trips there to shop and to have a meal out. Often, though, they go to town to hawk their handmade wares or the fruit in season. But rural people still observe many old traditions, customs and festivals which city people may have discarded, and these colour their lives.

Old folk in the countryside are often required to help out on the farm (above), and country homes lack modern conveniences, such as running water, so laundry is usually done by hand at a village pond, a lake or a river (right). Left and top: Workers tend to a vineyard, while a meal is prepared in a traditional kitchen.

*E*conomic reform has meant that farmers are now allowed to sell excess produce in the free market after selling the required quota to the government, and many are taking advantage of this ruling, for their produce fetch a better price in the free market. Clockwise from opposite left: A village seamstress; a bamboo ware seller; a vegetable farmer hawking produce from his farm; a street fruit-seller; a free market in Urumqi, Xinjiang; and a village meeting.

PART FOUR
ART AND ARCHITECTURE

C hina's artistic traditions go back thousands of years. Its earliest settlers along the Yellow River more than 7,000 years ago were making fine earthenware decorated with geometric and animal designs, while during the Shang dynasty, elaborate bronze vessels were used in ritual worship and burial. During the Tang dynasty, women were wearing jewellery and filigree hair ornaments made of gold and silver.

Silk, which was already in use during the Shang dynasty mainly as ceremonial garments, later became much sought after by Westerners and led to the rise of the Silk Road during the Han dynasty, through which trade in other goods between China and the West was also conducted. Cobalt blue from the Near East, which came via the Silk Road during the Yuan dynasty, was used to make blue and white porcelain, which then found its way back West. But before the invention of porcelain, lacquer was used to coat wooden food vessels such as plate and cups. Later, carved lacquer on a wooden base became popular as decorative pieces, and red lacquer pieces were given away as auspicious presents such as at weddings during the Ming and Qing dynasties.

By 600 B.C., the Chinese had begun to record music in notes, and music came to be an important part in their social life, being played at funerals and weddings alike. Ancient warriors charged into battle to the beat of drums, and in teahouses, songstresses accompanying themselves on the *pipa*, a lute, or accompanied by an old fiddler, entertained the guests. On festive occasions musicians were a must, and operas and dances, including the sinewy, vigorous lion and dragon dances of martial arts exponents, were also de rigueur.

The Chinese built walled cities to keep out enemies, sumptuous palaces and great temples. They sculpted figures of their gods and spirits to place in their temples and of mythical beasts to guard their homes and their dead. But they also carved intricate little figures of semi-precious stone and of wood to decorate their homes with or to carry in their sleeves.

Their scholar-administrators were also poets, calligraphers and painters. Their folk artists made woodcut prints of religious or mythological figures to put over the doors for luck, embroidered motifs of flowers on their clothes and shoes and created colourful dough dolls for the amusement of their children.

Chinese art styles have been copied by other people, such as the Japanese and Koreans, but the Chinese themselves have absorbed from those of others too. For example, designs for their blue and white porcelain were copied from Persian floral scrolls, and some of their musical instruments, such as the *pipa* and the *huqin*, a violin, came from Central Asia. Buddhist artistic tradition also influenced Chinese culture, and the Buddhist temple was the model for Chinese temples. In painting, Chinese artists have gone abroad to study Western art, and today, some painters blend the techniques of traditional Chinese painting with those of Western painting. Learning from others has enriched Chinese arts tremendously.

While ancient Daoist music has been lost elsewhere in the country, it is well-preserved by the Naxi minority group (left), who had imported the ritual music from Fujian and Sichuan provinces during the Ming dynasty for performance during their own religious occasions. Above: The Yellow Crane Tower in Wuhan, Hubei province, was built to commemorate a legend about a yellow crane and a tavern owner.

RELIGIOUS ART AND ARCHITECTURE

Chinese shrines can be as simple as a brass incense pot under a tree or a small altar, consisting of a portrait of a deity and an incense pot, placed in the living room. Or they may be huge complexes of buildings interspersed with fish ponds and rock gardens. Chinese temples are filled with statuary, from larger than life-size ones to those you can place on your palm, and their walls and ceilings are filled with paintings of scenes from religious tales or mythology. Beams and pillars are exposed and carved, and even roof ridges and the ends of circular roof tiles are carved with figures. Some of the earliest Buddhist temples in China, reflecting their Indian influence, are caves burrowed into hillsides, and filled with numerous carved Buddha images, as Buddhists believe it to be virtuous to multiply holy images.

Pagodas are sinicized versions of the Indian Buddhist stupa. The Dayan Pagoda (top), built during the Tang dynasty in present-day Xian (the ancient capital of the Tang and Han dynasties) and the graveyard of the famed Shaolin Monastery in Henan (facing page) are examples of the Indian influence. The Shaolin Monastery was founded in 495 and the 220 brick stupas of the graveyard date from the Tang to the Qing dynasty, containing remains of notable monks. Above: The Baoding or Precious stone carvings in Sichuan province were carved between 1179 and 1249, during the Yuan dynasty. Right: The Xuankong si, or Temple Suspended in a Void, perching on a cliff in the Heng Mountains in Shanxi province, was founded in the 6th century.

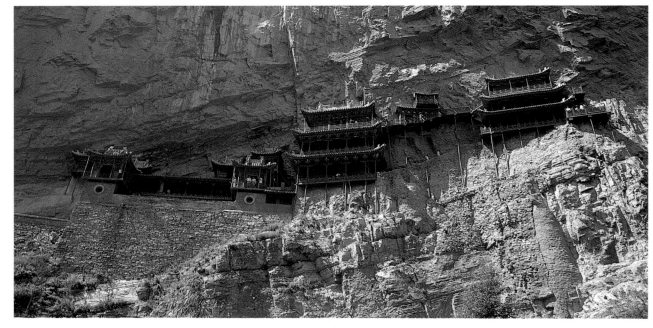

Buddhist Grottoes

There are several Buddhist cave temples throughout China, but the most important of these are the Thousand-Buddha Caves in Dunhuang, once an important centre of Buddhism at the edge of the Han dynasty domain, in present-day Gansu; Yungang Grottoes in Datong, an old frontier town near the Great Wall, in Shanxi province; and the Longmen Grottoes in Luoyang, an ancient capital of nine dynasties including the Tang, in northwest Henan.

The Dunhuang caves, carved out between the years 366 and 1000, number in the hundreds and are filled with wall paintings and stucco figures. The Longmen Grottoes, among the finest in China, were begun in 493, and carving continued into the Qing dynasty. The Yungang Grottoes are the earliest stone-carved caves in China, reflecting much Indian influence, although Chinese images are also found.

The Thousand-Buddha Caves in Dunhuang (top and centre left and right) were decorated with stucco figures and wall murals depicting scenes from the Jataka tales of the Buddha's life. The colours and styles suggest that Chinese artists were used. Above: A colossal seated Buddha at the Yungang Grottoes in Datong, an example of monumental Buddhist sculpture during the Northern Wei period.

Within the Temple of Heaven complex in Beijing, built during the Ming dynasty, is this Huangqiong yu, or Pavilion of the Sovereign Firmament, where the tablets of the imperial ancestors are kept (left). The blue roof (colour of the sky) and the circular shape are symbolic, as the Chinese traditionally believed that the heavens were circular. Far left and centre right: A building in the Nanputuo temple in Xiamen and the colourful Lama temple in Beijing sporting the traditional upturned eaves. Centre left and bottom: A jade Buddha image in a Shanghai temple and a reclining Buddha.

Temples

Chinese temples, like most Chinese buildings, are usually rectangular in shape, with roofs that have upturned eaves and elaborately decorated ridges, and surrounded by high walls. In front of the main entrance are a spirit wall, to ward off evil spirits, and usually a pair of stone lions standing guard. At the entrance are statues of four guardian gods, and beyond it is a courtyard, in the middle of which is a large incense urn and, in the case of Buddhist temples, pagodas.

The main hall holds an altar with the statue of the main deity in the centre and smaller statues of other deities at the sides, all framed by brightly embroidered brocade. Before the altar is the wooden altar table, elaborately carved, on which are placed incense urns, candle holders and offerings of food. Padded low stools in front of the altar are for devotees to kneel on as they pray. For the Buddhist temples, there would be Buddha images in the hall. Living quarters for temple-keepers and monks are usually at the back of the temple.

The dominant colours of Chinese temples are red, gold and green, to signify joy, heavenly glory and harmony respectively.

WALLED CITIES AND PALACES

To keep out invaders, the Chinese had built walled settlements from the Shang dynasty, sometimes surrounded by a moat. Most of these settlements kept to a rectangular plan, although in the hilly regions of the southeast, this was almost impossible. City walls were broad; for example, those of old Beijing were wide enough for several horsemen to ride abreast. Administrative buildings and palaces were usually located in the centre of the city, with a bell and a drum tower to announce the hours of the day and the opening and closing of the city gates. Most buildings, particularly in the north of China, were built facing south to avoid the cold winds from the north. Later, the south orientation of buildings became an important aspect of the Chinese art of building placement known as *feng shui* or "wind and water". Unfortunately, most Chinese buildings, even palaces, had a basic wooden frame, so few very old buildings have remained. But carvings in old imperial tombs showed that palaces were elaborate and sumptuous affairs.

Poets and painters have waxed lyrical about the Summer Palace in Beijing (facing page, top and above), which sits on a pretty 290-hectare site. Long an imperial residence, it was extended during the Qing dynasty by Emperor Qianlong. It was ransacked and destroyed in 1860 by British and French troops and rebuilt by the Dowager Empress Cixi in 1886. When it was destroyed again in 1900, she rebuilt it a second time, spending money the government could ill afford. She renamed it Yiheyuan or Garden of the Preservation of Harmony and spent her summers here. Left: The spirit way and entrance to the Ming tombs in Beijing. Right: The Qian Ling, tomb of the Tang emperor Gaozong and his empress Wu Zetian, 85 km northwest of Xian.

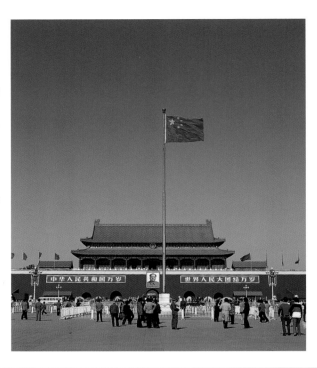

Forbidden City

At the heart of the old inner city of China's present-day capital, Beijing, is a group of imposing red-walled, gold-roofed buildings, surrounded by a moat and a high wall. This is the Zijincheng, or the Forbidden City, the imperial palace of the Ming and Qing dynasties, and home to the last Qing emperor, Xuantong, until 1924.

The front entrance to the palace, the Meridian gate, was used only by the emperor, and it was also from here that he reviewed his armies, passed judgement on prisoners and announced the new calendar for the year. The imposing main halls, raised on a balustraded marble terrace and overlooking a massive courtyard which can hold an imperial audience of 100,000, were where the emperor presided over matters of state. The first of these halls, the Hall of Supreme Harmony, is where the emperor's Dragon Throne sits. The emperor is associated with the dragon, and the dominant decorative figure here is the dragon. Behind the halls are the living quarters, on the western side of which are the palaces of the empress and concubines, decorated with phoenixes, the symbol of the empress. Domestic buildings are clustered round courtyards, which have a garden each. There are in all more than 800 buildings and 9,000 rooms.

The Wumen or Meridian Gate (left) is set in the thick walls of the Forbidden City itself, within the moat that surrounds the palace complex. The bronze lion (right) is one of a pair that guards the entrance of one of the palace buildings. It is a female lion; the male lion would have a ball under its front paw.

The inner courtyards (left and above) beyond the Hall of Preserving Harmony were the real "forbidden" city, as only eunuchs, maids and members of the imperial family could move freely here. Above centre: The entire Forbidden City complex is today known as the Palace Museum.

The Great Wall

Perhaps the greatest monument of China is the Great Wall, known as *the wanli changcheng* or "10,000 li fortification", which stretches over 10,000 km across northern China. It was begun in the Spring and Autumn period (770-476 B.C.) by feudal states to keep out invading tribes from the north. After unifying China in 221 B.C., Qin Shihuang linked up these walls into the Great Wall. Prisoners of war, convicts, civilians and farmers were press-ganged into building the wall, and many died of starvation and disease. Later dynasties added to the Wall. It starts on the east coast at Shanhaiguan Pass, crosses loess plateaus, mountains, deserts and lush valleys, and ends at Jiayuguan Pass in the Gobi desert, passing through five provinces and two autonomous regions. Parts of the wall are broad enough for 10 soldiers to walk abreast and rise to a height of nine metres.

HOUSES AND GARDENS

The traditional Chinese house is a cluster of buildings grouped around a series of courtyards and surrounded by a high wall to afford privacy. Just within the main entrance of the house, which usually faces south, is a spirit wall to ward off evil spirits which are believed to be able to move only in straight lines. Main buildings face south and less important buildings are arranged on either side of these, facing into the courtyard. The first building facing the entrance usually houses the reception room and an ancestral shrine. Inner buildings are private apartments, with the head of the household living in the main building and servants and children in side buildings. Round moon gates connect the different courtyards. Chinese houses usually have gardens in the courtyards, with small ones perhaps sporting a rockery with a tree or two and enormous affairs complete with streams big enough for small boats to pass, pools with their own viewing pavilions and even artificial hills with hollowed out caves.

A Chinese Courtyard

Being in a Chinese courtyard garden is like being in a painting that has come alive. Courtyard gardens are designed to be viewed from a framed opening. There is usually a covered corridor that runs round the garden, which has a series of latticed windows. Walking down the corridor and looking through the windows, one sees perhaps a bamboo grove or a wisteria or a carefully placed rock, a series of pictures set in motion as one moves. Thus, walking round the garden is like being in a painting whose scene changes with the viewer's movement. Pavilions are built at various points from which to enjoy the garden over tea or wine, particularly over a pool where one can view the reflections of the garden or the silvery moon of an evening. Some of the most beautiful courtyard gardens can be found in Suzhou.

Chinese build pavilions everywhere, in their gardens and parks, on hillsides and hilltops or just by a footpath, at which to rest one's feet and take in the surrounding view. The Poem Reciting Pavilion by the East Lake in Wuhan (facing page, top), the Black Dragon Pool in Lijiang, Yunnan (top left), and the Humble Administrator's Garden in Suzhou (left and above right). Rockeries and pengzhai, miniaturized trees and plants in pots (top right) are elements of the Chinese courtyard garden.

Wind and Water

Be it a city, a house or a tomb, the Chinese choose its site very carefully in accordance with the principles of *feng shui*, or "wind and water", the orientation of buildings in relation to the natural elements of winds (*feng*) and waters (*shui*), hills and valleys.

The Chinese believe that streams of *qi* or "cosmic breath" run through the earth, and it is important to avoid bad *qi*, at the same time tap the good *qi* of a site, which will influence the fortunes of the building's occupants. In the case of a tomb, its siting will influence the fortunes of the deceased's descendants.

Some general rules of thumb are that there should be hills to the north and water to the south, and that buildings should face south, with the protective hills behind them. It is therefore not for nothing that Chinese tombs are built on hillsides. A geomancer is consulted before a building is put up, and, using a geomancer's compass and taking note of the owner's birth date and time, he would determine whether a site is good and what elements the building should have to make best use of its *qi*.

A TOUCH OF THE WEST

Shanghai was known as the Paris of the East during the 1930s, and evidence of the dominance of the small but powerful Western population during the turn of the century is still found in the buildings of that era that still stand in what were the International Settlement and the French Concession. On the Bund, the waterfront, are the imposing office buildings of the major hongs, or Western companies, built in the style of the buildings of their countries of origin. Moving westwards, beyond several big department stores, one sees large apartment blocks built in the Art Deco styles of the 20s and 30s. These in turn give way to the mansions of the old taipans, the big men who ran the powerful business houses, which range in style from the Gothic to the Tudor. There are also villas in the French, Spanish and English styles and Gothic churches. Elsewhere in China, European-style buildings can be found from that era, such as German houses in Shandong province where the Germans had a strong presence.

During the late 19th and early 20th century, the Chinese government was forced to open its ports and grant concessions to Western powers, and a legacy of this period of Chinese history is the architecture of these foreigners. Facing page: A hunting lodge (top left) and the Qingdao railway station (centre) built in German colonial style; a red-brick building in Guangzhou (top right); and a French Catholic church in Tianjin (bottom). This page: Scenes of Shanghai — buildings on the Bund (above); the Stock Exchange building (left); and the Oriental Pearl TV Tower (top).

ART AND THE ARTIST

With a strong literary tradition, it was inevitable that painting and calligraphy, artistic expressions closely linked to it, became the dominant visual arts of China. Painting was pursued by both professional and scholar-painters. The professional painter, trained in portrait and decorative painting, produced works intended for private homes, palaces and temples, and worked in ateliers, while the scholar-painter, a member of the educated class, learnt calligraphy and painting as part of his education. Usually an administrator who had passed the imperial examinations, he painted mainly in his spare time and did not sell his works, but gave them away to friends as gifts.

Many Chinese painters and poets sought inspiration from nature, and travelled long distances to visit China's famous mountains and rivers to lose themselves amid the clouds, trees, rocks and flowing waters. Once, the great calligrapher Wang Xizhi (321-379) organized a party by a pond in the country, where the men floated cups of wine on the pool's surface, and whenever a cup stopped before one of them, he had to compose a poem or pay the penalty of drinking the wine. Wine has always been associated with the arts in China, and poets, painters and calligraphers produced some of their best works under its influence.

The age-old tradition of writing auspicious spring couplets for hanging on doorways during the spring festival or Lunar New Year (right) has survived, even as artists have adopted Western art styles such as painting with oils (above and top).

Calligraphy — Rhythms and Forms

The great calligrapher Wang Xizhi once wrote of his art: "Every horizontal stroke is like a mass of clouds in battle formation, every hook like a bent bow of the greatest strength, every dot like a falling rock from a high peak, every turning of the stroke like a brass hook, every drawn-out line like a dry vine of great old age, and every swift and free stroke like a runner on his start." The Chinese art of writing derives its inspiration from the rhythms and forms of nature. Its lines may be forceful, supple, graceful, rugged or delicate, and its form irregular or proportional, harmonious or contrasting. Although calligraphers reproduce poems, couplets or proverbs in their works, their meanings are usually forgotten and the lines and forms are appreciated in themselves. Calligraphy is regarded as a form of self-cultivation and self-expression, and a person's calligraphy reflects his character, and conveys feelings which sometimes words cannot.

Chinese place a great importance on calligraphy and children are trained from young to write a good hand. There are several forms of calligraphy including the chao shu, *or grass writing, so named because the characters look like wind-blown grass. The tools of calligraphy are simple, consisting of brush, ink stick, inkstone and paper, known collectively as the* wenfangsibao *or "four treasures of the study". Calligraphers at work (above and top), carving calligraphy on stone (top right) and brushes in a shop window (right).*

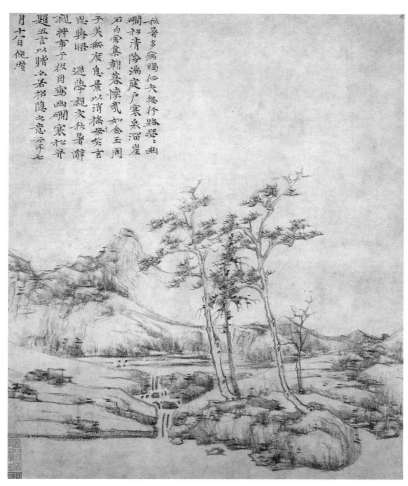

Masters of the Brush

It is often said that Chinese calligraphy provides the aesthetic basis for Chinese painting, and indeed, Chinese calligraphers first mastered the use of brush and ink, with the painters adopting these skills to create their art. Chinese painters began by painting themes from myth and history, then moved on to a more poetic expression in landscape painting. They also painted subjects such as flowers, birds, animals, fish and insects. During the Tang dynasty, there emerged a more spontaneous, allusive and calligraphic style of landscape painting, in which only ink was used and details were left out, which came to be favoured by scholar-painters. A new form of court painting developed during the Song dynasty in which subjects such as birds and flowers were painted in minute detail using bright, jewel-like colours, and which was to exert an influence on Chinese painting even to this day. Chan Buddhist and Daoist styles of painting were also influential, particularly in the use of strong, bold strokes. In more recent times, Chinese artists have travelled abroad, to Japan and Europe, and many European-inspired experiments have been tried out. Today, some painters blend the techniques of traditional Chinese painting with those of Western painting.

In the past, portrait painting was usually done by professional painters, who would be commissioned to paint royalty and nobility (left), and they used a lot of detail and colour in their works, which were usually unsigned. But scholar-painters favoured ink painting, in a minimalist style, partly to distinguish their works from those of the professional painters (top left). It is a tradition to inscribe paintings, showing who owned them and what the owners thought of them. Top right: The tiger is one of the favourite subjects of Chinese painters. Above: A contemporary painter who has incorporated some elements of traditional Chinese painting in his works.

CRAFTS

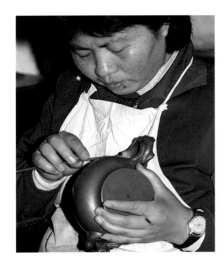

Chinese crafts have been the domain of folk artists and artisans who make utensils into objects of beauty. Through history, craftsmen worked in government workshops as potters, bronze casters and carvers, turning out handsome chariots, fine porcelain vessels, lacquerware and jade ornaments for royalty and nobility, while folk artists made everyday ceramics, baskets, festival lanterns and woven goods, and carved furniture and woodblocks to print festive New Year pictures, for use of the common people. Their crafts may be differ-

ent, but they used, and still do, similar motifs and symbols from nature, myth and history to decorate their objects. Peach is used to symbolize longevity while bamboo, because they bend in the wind but always return to an upright position, to symbolize resilience and integrity. Images of myth include the monkey spirit and Chang Er, the woman believed to live on the moon. These crafts are still being made today, some recreation of old pieces while some are new interpretations of traditional styles. While old motifs and symbols are still being used, there are also new ones to reflect the new society.

As the ancients have done through the ages, craftsmen across China today work in workshops turning out decorative and functional objects: Putting the finishing touches on a clay teapot at Yixing, where the first potteries were built during the 16th century (top left); carving a red lacquer vase in Yangzhou (above); and painting ceramic figures (left) and paper fans (right). Top right: A blue cloisonne vase.

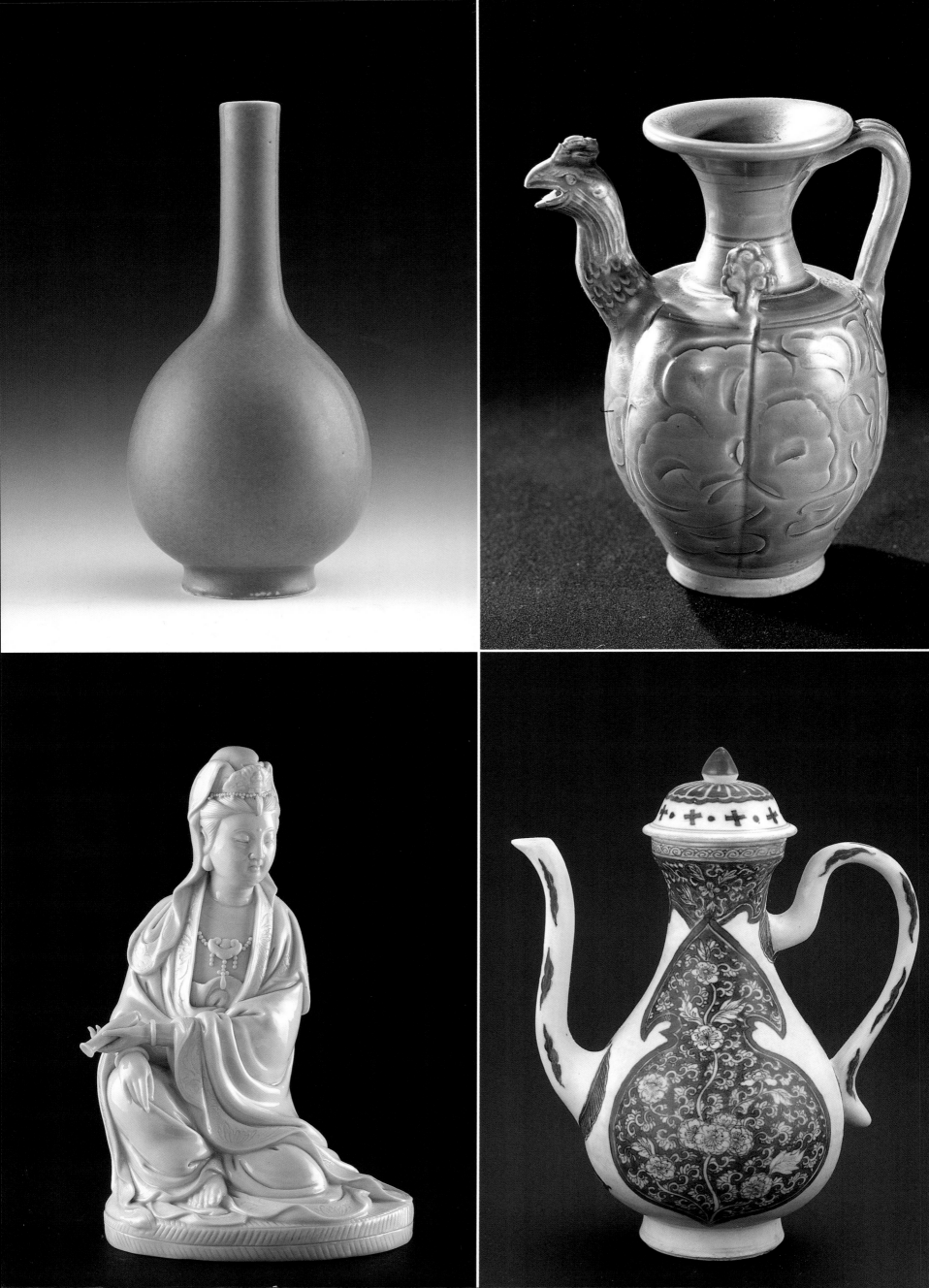

Ceramics

Ceramics have been in used in China in daily life since 7,000 years ago. The earliest were earthenware decorated with black geometric and animal designs. During the Shang dynasty, clay began to be used, which were partially glazed with a transparent glaze. By the Han dynasty, green glazes were used, and ceramics were used in burials, the way bronzes were during the Shang period. Models of houses, granaries, farmyards complete with domestic animals, and human figures were buried with the dead.

Around the 7th century, a white clay was discovered on the banks of the Yellow and Yangzi rivers, and thus was white porcelain born. Porcelain was used to make containers for food and drink, and by the Tang dynasty, porcelain ware was being exported in large quantities to as far as Egypt and the African coast. The most celebrated of Chinese porcelain must be the blue and white porcelain of the Yuan and Ming dynasty, exported in large quantities to the West, and giving rise to the use of the term "china" to describe porcelain. During the Qing dynasty, however, the full five-colour palette was used on porcelain, as Manchus loved bright colours.

Ceramic funerary objects dug out from ancient tombs reveal the way of life of the people then. This page, clockwise from top: Ceramic funerary objects from the Tang dynasty of servants bearing a sedan and a Tang court lady; an earthen receptacle; and a drummer on a camel. Facing page, clockwise from top left: Antique porcelains — a pink vase; a wine carafe from the Song dynasty; a blue-and-white wine pot; and a white figurine of the Guan Yin, the Buddhist Goddess of Mercy.

Art of Embroidery

It is likely that embroidery arose with the discovery of silk, with silk thread being used to embroider colourful motifs of flowers, butterflies and geometric designs on clothes, shoes, fans and purses. Embroidery was also used to decorate household items such as wall hangings, bedspreads and tablecloths. It has always been women's work, and in the olden days, girls were trained from young to embroider. Items such as children's clothing and women's skirts, jackets, parasols, shawls, slippers and purses were embroidered at home. In poor families a skilled embroiderer could work from home on jobs farmed out by private and imperial workshops, and upon marriage, a woman who brought good embroidery skill to her new home was accorded a higher status than otherwise. Besides being used as decoration, embroidery has also been refined into an art, in the delicate embroidered painting on silk or gauze. Some of these paintings can be viewed from both sides.

A Qing dynasty woman's tunic is decorated with phoenixes and peonies and children's hats and shoes with tiger and mouse motifs (left). Phoenix and dragon motifs (top) were used only on robes of members of the imperial family.
Above: Young girls at a Shanghai children's palace learning to embroider.
Right: Peasant embroidery being sold by street traders.

THE PERFORMING ARTS

Music traditionally played an important part in Chinese social life, so it is no wonder that the first drama to develop in China, beginning in the Yuan dynasty, was the opera. It is still a popular form of entertainment, although it is fast being overshadowed by modern forms of entertainment, especially among young people.

The spoken drama came to China in the early 1900s and had always been used to support causes. It was at first used to fight feudalistic ways, and later for communist propaganda. Today, plays examine more personal themes such as love and betrayal and social problems brought about by the new materialism.

Cinema came to China in the wake of the spoken drama, in the 1920s, and early Chinese movies were very much influenced by Russian cinema and by Hollywood. Chinese cinema went through a low point during the Cultural Revolution, and started to flourish again in the 1980s. The first movies to emerge then reflected the directors' rural experiences during the Cultural Revolution, but later movies began to examine the new urban lifestyle of the Chinese. Some of these movies have won international acclaim.

In the past, storytelling (such as this above) was a favourite form of street entertainment, especially of illiterate peasants, who would pay a small fee to be enthralled by animated recounting of heroic deeds taken from epics such as The Romance of the Three Kingdoms *and the* Water Margin. *Today, it is a dying art.*

Another popular street entertainment of old is the puppet opera, complete with its own musicians (above). Groups of musicians like this one (right) enjoying a jam session are commonly seen in China, whether at a teahouse, in the park or outside someone's house. Above right: Young dancers performing a patriotic dance.

There has been a revival of the cinema and stage since the end of the Cultural Revolution in 1976, with a burgeoning body of new work, some of which have travelled well abroad. A movie being shot (top left) and Gong Li (top right), perhaps the best-known screen actress outside of China, in the award-winning movie To Live. Above: The staging of the Chinese American play, Joy Luck Club, by a Shanghai theatre group.

Opera — Street Entertainment

Chinese opera began as street entertainment, and loud gongs, cymbals and drums were used to attract an audience. There are today 300 forms of traditional opera in China, the more widely popular

ones being Beijing, Yue, Ping and Yu. The opera stage is usually quite bare except for a painted backdrop and some pieces of furniture, usually stools and tables. But actors are dressed colourfully in glittering costume and headdress and heavily made up. An actor's make-up tells the audience whether his or her character is upright or dishonest, cruel or kind, a tragic figure or a clown. Much of the action is mimed, such as mounting a horse or opening a door, and most of the dialogue is sung. Martial arts and acrobatics are also used, for battle and fight scenes. Stories are taken from historical epics, folk legends, classical novels or fairytales, and may be comic or tragic. Audiences are noisy, discussing the action loudly, passing round food and drinks, and shouting *hao* or "good" when they approve of a particular performance.

In the past, only men performed in the opera, playing both male and female roles. Opera actors had very low status in society and relied very much on the patronage of the rich. Only the poor who could not afford food for their child would apprentice him to an opera troupe. Different regions have their own operas, each with its own style and strengths; for instance, Beijing opera (facing page, top left and above) stresses acrobatics and martial combat. Left: Performance of a Ping opera, one of the most popular opera forms today.

Acrobatics

Acrobatics started out as a means of livelihood for farmers during the winter months, which explains why props used are usually household items such as crockery and chairs. Women might spin several plates on the ends of sticks at the same time, or balance bowls on a stick clenched between the teeth while turning and twisting the body, while men balance on chairs piled precariously one on top of the other. There are also contortionist acts, and performing animals are popular as well.

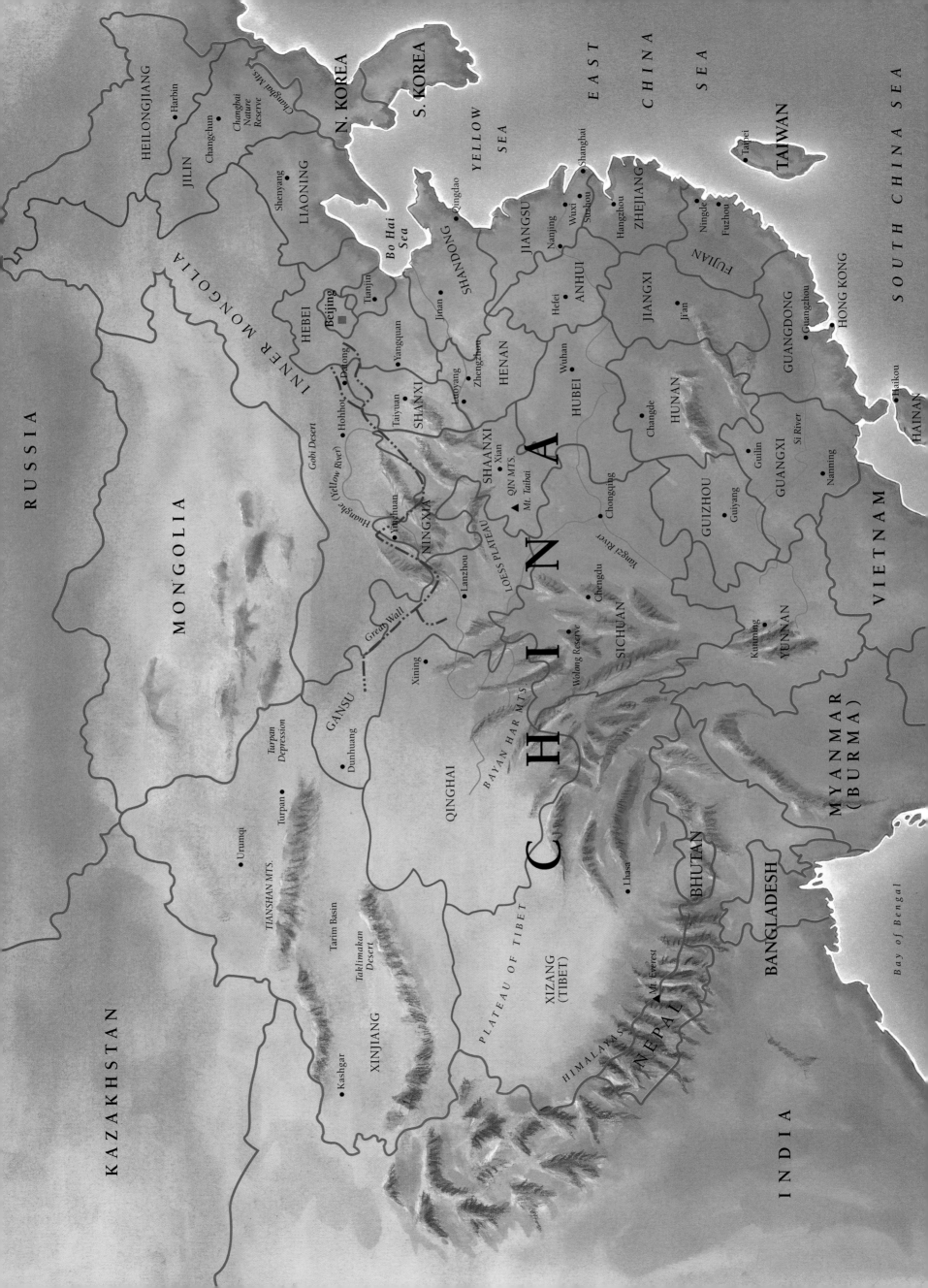

RUSSIA

KAZAKHSTAN

HEILONGJIANG

•Harbin

JILIN

Changchun•

Changbai Nature Reserve

Changbai Mts.

N. KOREA

S. KOREA

LIAONING

Shenyang•

Bo Hai Sea

YELLOW SEA

EAST CHINA SEA

TAIWAN

•Taipei

INNER MONGOLIA

MONGOLIA

Gobi Desert

Huanghe (Yellow River)

Datong•
Hohhot•

Beijing■
Tianjin•

HEBEI

Yangquan•

Taiyuan•
SHANXI

Yinchuan•
NINGXIA

Lanzhou•

SHAANXI

Xian•

QIN MTS.
▲ Mt. Taibai

LOESS PLATEAU

Jinan•
SHANDONG

Qingdao•

Zhengzhou•
Leoyang•
HENAN

Wuhan•
HUBEI

NANJING•
Nanjing•
JIANGSU

Wuxi•
Suzhou•
Hangzhou•
Shanghai•

ZHEJIANG

ANHUI

Hefei•

Ningde•
Fuzhou•

FUJIAN

JIANGXI

Jian•

SOUTH CHINA SEA

GUANGDONG

Guangzhou•

HONG KONG

Haikou•
HAINAN

C H I N A

Xining•

GANSU

Dunhuang•

QINGHAI

Great Wall

BAYAN HAR MTS.

Changde•
HUNAN

Chongqing•

Chengdu•
SICHUAN

Wolong Reserve•

Yangzi River

Guilin•
GUIZHOU

Guiyang•

GUANGXI

Si River

Nanning•

Kunming•
YUNNAN

VIETNAM

URUMQI
Urumqi•

TIANSHAN MTS.

Turpan Depression

Turpan•

Tarim Basin

Taklimakan Desert

XINJIANG

Kashgar•

PLATEAU OF TIBET

XIZANG (TIBET)

Lhasa•

BHUTAN

Mt. Everest
▲
HIMALAYAS
NEPAL

BANGLADESH

MYANMAR (BURMA)

Bay of Bengal

INDIA

CHINA
IN PAINT AND PRINT

A section of the wall murals in the tomb of the Tang princess Yongtai, who is said to have been murdered by her own mother Empress Wu Zetian, showing a group of female attendants bearing offerings, candles and flowers. Almost life-sized, the women are depicted in loose groups moving towards the site of the coffin. These wall paintings give a clue to the style of court painting of that period, which was probably racy, lively and colourful.

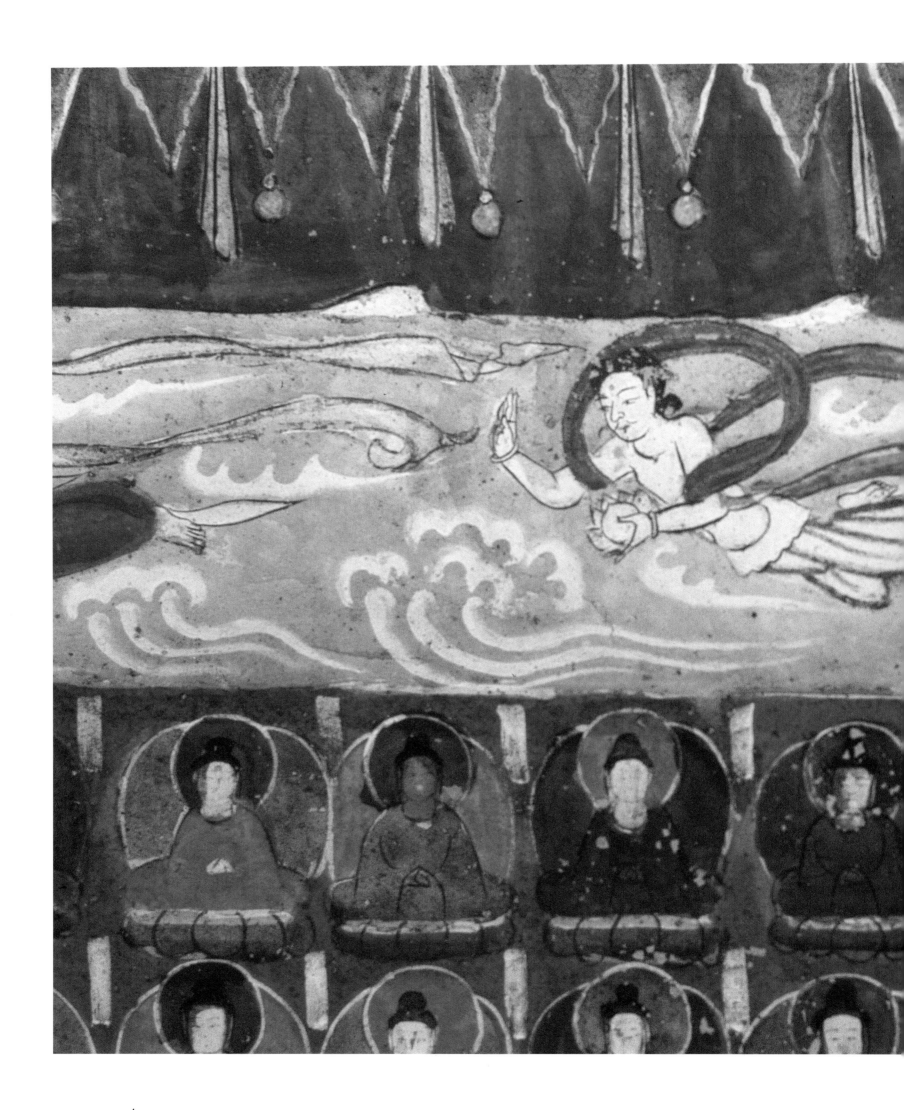

A Buddhist wall mural from the period of the Tang empress Wu Zetian's reign (624-705), in which the Buddha images bear womanish facial features. It was during her reign that religious art became more feminine and bodhisattvas were feminized, with the Bodhisattva Avalokitesvara, or Guan Yin the Goddess of Mercy, given a female form.

*W*all paintings of the Tashilhunpo Monastery in Shigatse, Tibet, built in the 15th century (preceding spread), the Palkhor Monastery in Gyantze (above) and the Summer Palace in Lhasa (right). Besides depicting Buddha images and scenes from the Buddha's life, Tibetan Buddhist paintings also depict fiercer images of Tibetan Buddhism, such as Yama, the bull-headed God of Death, and Lha Mo the Terrible Goddess. Tibetan Buddhism is a mix of Indian Buddhism — introduced in the 7th century supposedly by the Tang princess Wen Cheng who married the Tibetan king Songtsang Kampo — and the local religion of Bon, the worship of nature, which combined shamanism with astrology and magic.

*F*rench paintings of the landscape in the southwestern province of Yunnan (left) and of the local tribal people
(above). The French came to Yunnan during the 19th century via Indo-China, which they had by then subjugated.
Keen to exploit the copper, lumber and tin resources in Yunnan, they built a railway from Vietnam to Kunming, the
capital of Yunnan. Today, French-influenced architecture can still be seen in Kunming.

*B*lack and white prints from the Qing dynasty period of a court official (above) and of a family at leisure (right). Women, particularly of the upper classes, smoked water pipes, such as the one smoked by the woman at right, and opium, like the men. The dispute over the sale of opium by the British to the Chinese led to the damaging Opium Wars in the latter half of the 19th century, which resulted in the defeat of the Chinese and the signing of unequal treaties between them and the British and other foreign powers.

*P*ropaganda posters of the earlier Communist period extolling the virtues of putting money in the bank (left, top) and of earnest workers learning from the little Red Book containing Mao's thoughts, the "bible" of the Red Guards during the Cultural Revolution (left, bottom). Such propaganda posters can still be seen today, such as those urging people to plan their family or make advances in science and technology. Above: A portrait of Mao Zedong. Mao iconography was a rage during the 1980s and the 1990s.

*L*ively renditions of the Laughing Buddha (above) and of the Daoist god Zhongkui (right). Both Chan Buddhist and Daoist painting are characterized by the use of bold strokes. Chan Buddhist paintings are witty and humorous and, like Daoist paintings, display great spontaneity, perhaps because Chan Buddhists believe in sudden enlightenment.

A folk art piece depicting the preparation of a feast. Chinese folk art is characterized by the use of brilliant colours and romantic forms and of light brush strokes. Folk art usually depicts joy and festivity, as in the New Year paintings used by farmers as festive decoration.

翠之士　張迅君即屬其二君於篆隸行草

惠智公嘗語魯公嘗以楷法劉正厚重冠絕古

於五代之楊凝式遊之如隋李之錢南園

大家今觀君作此冊楷書正氣歛大

年葓護斯造指誠不易得如磨而

月曩戢因將付梓窗為之序矣慶慶